THE RICH CAB DRIVER

THE UNTOLD STORY OF HOW A CAB DRIVER BECAME A MILLIONAIRE

(BASED ON A TRUE STORY)

ALLEN BROWN

CREATOR OF THE FIVE-FOLD WEALTH SYSTEM

BUILD OUR KINGDOM PUBLISHING

BUILD OUR KINGDOM.COM

The Rich Cab Driver

Published by Build Our Kingdom Publishing, LLC

Printed in the United States of America

1st Edition March 2025 First Printing
ISBN for paperback: 978-1-964203-28-7
Build Our Kingdom Publishing, LLC. 560 Main St, Stroudsburg, PA 18360
Edited by: Allen Brown

Table of Contents

Dedication

This book is dedicated to those who have pushed past the limitations of believing that college was the only path to success. It is for the dreamers, the risk-takers, and the ones who dared to explore a different way. May this book serve as a testament that success is not limited to a single route, but is available to those who are willing to learn, take action, and create their own opportunities. If you believe in yourself and trust the process, you can achieve more than you ever imagined.

~ Allen Brown ~

Acknowledgment

First and foremost, I thank God, whose wisdom, grace, and divine guidance have shaped my journey. I acknowledge every mentor who took the time to share knowledge, every banker and loan officer who believed in my vision, and every landlord and investor who played a role in my growth.

To everyone who has pushed, supported, or even doubted me—thank you. Your presence, in one way or another, has contributed to the story written in these pages. Every deal I made, every lesson I learned, and every challenge I faced led me to where I am today.

This book is a testament to what's possible when you keep moving forward, trust in the process, and never stop learning.

Introduction

The Path Most Travelled—And the One Less Taken

Every day, countless people wake up, go to work, and follow a path they never truly chose for themselves. They were programmed from childhood to believe in a system—a system that promises stability but rarely delivers true freedom. From an early age, they were asked, "What do you want to be when you grow up?"—as if their entire identity and future could be neatly packaged into a single career title. The answers are predictable: doctor, lawyer, engineer, police officer, athlete. These responses aren't entirely their own. They are echoes of what they've heard, what they've been conditioned to believe is possible, acceptable, and respectable.

But what if there was another way?

This is the story of two friends, Sam and Derrick, who grew up in the same neighborhood, shared the same childhood experiences, and had similar ambitions. Both were taught the same lessons about success: Get an education. Find a good job. Work hard. Retire. Society's formula for a "good life" was instilled in them from the very beginning.

Derrick followed this formula precisely. He pursued higher education, obtained multiple degrees, and secured a corporate job that society deemed prestigious. Yet, despite all his efforts, he found himself caught in the same struggles as millions of others—long hours, financial limitations, and a life that felt more like a routine than a dream fulfilled.

Sam, on the other hand, saw things differently. He couldn't shake the feeling that something was off—that the very system designed to create "success" was, in reality, a trap. He questioned why people spent the best years of their lives chasing security rather than freedom. He rejected the notion that a degree was the only ticket to wealth and, instead, took a leap of faith in an unconventional direction.

He became a cab driver.

That decision alone should have sealed his fate as someone who would "never make it." After all, who chooses driving a cab over climbing the corporate ladder? Who walks away from the security of a degree, a salary, and a retirement plan?

But that's exactly what makes Sam's story different. He didn't just drive a cab—he leveraged it. He turned an everyday job into an empire, proving that success isn't about titles or degrees—it's about choices, strategy, and understanding how money truly works.

This book is about two lives shaped by two different belief systems. Sam, who defied societal expectations and found financial freedom beyond what anyone could have imagined.

And Derrick, who did everything "right" yet found himself trapped in an invisible cycle—earning well but never truly wealthy, following the rules yet never quite free.

Why did Sam's path lead to wealth while Derrick's led to mediocrity?

How did less education give Sam an advantage over Derrick, who pursued more?

What was the key decision that separated their fates?

This is more than just a story. It's an awakening. A challenge to everything you've been told about success.

Because the truth is—what you believe about wealth may be the very thing keeping you from it.

Chapter 1

The Decision That Changed Everything

The night of graduation was full of celebration. Families gathered, cameras flashed, and a sense of accomplishment filled the air. Sam and Derrick had just crossed a major milestone in their lives, completing twelve years of school with the world ahead of them. Their parents beamed with pride, their friends talked about their plans, and everywhere they turned, people kept repeating the same phrase:

"The future is yours."

But for Sam, that phrase felt more like a question.

The next day, while most of their classmates were still soaking in the excitement of graduation, Sam and Derrick met up at their favorite hangout spot—a small park near their neighborhood, sitting on the same swings they had played on as kids. It was the perfect place to talk about the future, though Sam wasn't sure what he had to say.

Derrick leaned back, looking over at Sam. "So, what's the plan, man?"

Sam shrugged. "I don't know yet."

Derrick's eyes widened. "What do you mean you don't know? Bro, it's college. What else is there? You have to go. You know what can happen if you don't?"

Sam smirked. “Nah, tell me.”

Derrick scoffed. “How are you going to get a good job? How are you going to take care of yourself? Your family? Everybody knows college is the way to go. You get your degree, you get a career, and you’re set for life.”

Sam sighed, kicking the dirt beneath his feet. “That’s what everybody says. But I don’t know, man… something about it doesn’t sit right with me.”

Derrick shook his head. “What’s not sitting right? Education is the key to success.”

Sam chuckled. “Yeah? My parents have degrees. Multiple ones. And I still hear them stress about money every day. I see them struggle. So, if education is the key, why hasn’t it unlocked their freedom?”

Derrick was quiet for a moment, then shrugged. “At least they have those degrees. You don’t want to be left behind, man.”

Sam sighed again. “But what if college isn’t for me? What if I waste years studying something I don’t even care about? What if I’m just following the same path as everybody else without even questioning if it’s the right one?”

Derrick frowned. “So what are you going to do instead? Just sit around?”

Sam didn’t have an answer. But deep down he had faith in God that all things would work out for him. He just didn’t know how.

The Road Less Traveled

By the end of the summer, Derrick packed his bags and headed off to college. Sam, on the other hand, stayed behind.

And for the first time in his life, he felt alone.

His parents were disappointed. His friends were gone. Everywhere he turned, people kept asking, "So, when are you starting school?"

Sam didn't have an answer for them either.

He needed to make money, but with no degree and no clear direction, his job options were limited. He ended up delivering pizzas at a local shop, a job that paid the bills but felt far from any kind of future. It wasn't glamorous, and it certainly wasn't what his parents had envisioned for him.

But this job, as simple as it seemed, would change his life forever.

A New Perspective

One night, after a long shift of deliveries, Sam returned to the pizza shop just as the owner, Tony, was closing up. Tony, a gruff but friendly guy in his forties, was stacking empty pizza boxes for the next day.

"You need help with that?" Sam asked.

Tony, who usually declined, paused for a moment before nodding. "Yeah, actually. Why not?"

As they folded boxes, Sam found himself opening up. "You ever feel like you're just going through the motions, but you don't really know where you're going?"

Tony chuckled. "Every day when I was your age."

Sam glanced at him. "Really? You didn't go to college?"

Tony shook his head. "Nope."

Sam was surprised. "Then how'd you end up owning this place?"

Tony leaned against the counter, wiping his hands. "I figured something out early. College wasn't the only way to get an education."

Sam frowned. "What do you mean?"

Tony smirked. "People think a degree is the only way to get smart, but what does it really do? It qualifies you—to work for somebody else."

Sam's eyebrows furrowed. "What do you mean 'qualifies you to work for someone else'?"

Tony pointed at him. "Think about it. You go to school, spend thousands of dollars, learn how to do a job… but who benefits? The companies that hire you. They don't pay you based on how smart you are. They pay you based on how much they can profit from your work. That's why salaries have limits, but business owners don't."

Sam's mouth dropped slightly. He had never thought about it like that.

"So you never regretted not going to college?" he asked.

Tony chuckled. "Not for a second. I took what little money I had, learned how to run a business, and now I work for myself. More importantly, I don't have to ask someone else for permission to make money."

Sam sat back. For the first time since graduation, he felt a sense of clarity.

This conversation was the first time someone had told him that freedom wasn't just about money—it was about control.

Tony's words sparked something in him. He didn't fully understand it yet, but he could feel it—he was seeing the world differently.

And from that moment on, he would never think about success the same way again. Tony and Sam spent many more nights talking and Sam continued to soke up the information

End of Chapter One: The Spark of an Idea

Sam had just met his first mentor.

A pizza shop owner.

A man who didn't have a degree.

A man who thought differently.

And for the first time in his life, Sam didn't feel guilty about his decision to skip college.

Instead, he felt like he had made the first real choice of his own.

Little did he know, this was just the beginning.

Biblical Perspective From the Author: The Power of Decisions and Faith

Sam's decision to forgo the traditional path of college in pursuit of financial independence mirrors the biblical principle of seeking wisdom over worldly expectations. Proverbs 3:5-6 (NIV) reminds us: *"Trust in the Lord with all your heart and lean not on your own understanding; in all your ways submit to Him, and He will make your paths straight."* Sam chose to trust his instincts and explore a different path, just as many biblical figures, like Abraham and David, trusted God's direction over societal norms.

The story of Joseph in Genesis also highlights that success isn't always tied to a conventional route. Despite setbacks, Joseph's faith and wisdom led him to a position of great influence. Like Sam, your path to success may not look like everyone else's, but by seeking wisdom, taking bold steps, and trusting in God's plan, you can unlock the doors to financial and spiritual prosperity.

The Power of Divine Connections

Sam's encounter with Tony, the pizza shop owner, was no coincidence. It was a divine appointment that introduced him to a new way of thinking. Proverbs 13:20 (NIV) says, "Walk with the wise and become wise, for a companion of fools suffers harm." The people we surround ourselves with shape our mindset and influence our future.

In the Bible, we see how divine connections changed lives—like when Moses met Jethro, who gave him wisdom on leadership (Exodus 18:17-24) or when Elijah mentored Elisha, preparing him for greater things (2 Kings 2:9-10).

Sam's journey reminds us that God often places the right people in our path to challenge our thinking, provide wisdom, and open doors we never imagined. The key is to remain open, willing to listen, and humble enough to learn. Your success may not come from where you expect, but God will always align you with the right people if you seek Him first.

Chapter 1 Notes

- What stood out to you in this chapter?
- How can you apply these principles to your own life?
- What action steps will you take moving forward?

Chapter 2

Life Comes Fast

Sam never expected his life to take a turn so quickly.

It all started one random night at work. He was delivering pizza, just like any other day, when he knocked on the door of a small apartment complex. The door swung open, and standing there was Karen—a young woman with a bright smile, playful eyes, and an energy that immediately caught his attention.

She glanced at his uniform and smirked. "Well, aren't you a cute pizza guy?"

Sam laughed, caught off guard. "Uh… thanks? Here's your order."

Karen took the pizza, still eyeing him with curiosity. "You always deliver around here?"

Sam nodded. "Yeah, part of the job."

She leaned against the doorframe. "Well, if I keep ordering pizza, does that mean I'll get to see you again?"

That was all it took. One night turned into texts, texts turned into dates, and before Sam knew it, he and Karen were officially together.

For a while, life felt good. She was fun, she was exciting, and for the first time since graduation, Sam wasn't thinking about what he didn't have—he was just enjoying the moment.

Reality Hits Hard

A year and a half later, reality hit like a brick wall.

Karen was pregnant.

Sam sat on his bed that night, staring at the ceiling, feeling like the weight of the world had just landed on his chest. He wasn't even sure where his life was going—how was he supposed to be a father?

When their son was born, something changed. He loved his child more than he thought possible, but everything else in his life felt like it was falling apart.

Karen wasn't happy. Sam wasn't making enough money. They started fighting—a lot.

"You're still delivering pizzas, Sam! How are we supposed to survive on that?"

"I'm trying, Karen! What do you want me to do?"

"I want you to step up! Get a real job! Do something!"

The arguments became daily. Eventually, Karen left.

Now, Sam was a single dad—still living with his parents, still delivering pizzas, and feeling completely stuck.

The pressure was unbearable. His parents helped where they could, but deep down, he knew they were disappointed. This wasn't the future they had imagined for their son.

One night, after a particularly exhausting day, Sam sat alone in his car, gripping the steering wheel, staring out into the dark streets.

"Is this my life?"

"Is this all I'm going to be?"

The Park Bench Talk

A few months later, Derrick came home for a visit. It was his last year of college, and he had big plans.

"Yo, let's meet up," Derrick had texted.

And just like old times, they found themselves at their spot in the park, sitting on the swings, just like they had the day after graduation.

Derrick leaned back, stretching his arms. "Man, it feels good to be back. Crazy how much things have changed, huh?"

Sam let out a dry chuckle. "Yeah. Real crazy."

Derrick glanced at him. "So, what's been up with you? Still at the pizza place?"

Sam exhaled. "Yeah. But, uh… I've also got a kid now."

Derrick's eyes widened. "Wait, what?"

"Yeah, man. His name's Malik. He's almost a year old now."

Derrick shook his head, clearly shocked. "Damn, bro. I didn't know… So, you and his mom…?"

Sam shook his head. "Nah. It didn't work out."

A long silence followed. The weight of their different lives hung between them.

Derrick finally spoke. "Man… I have to be honest. You're better than this, Sam. You should've come to college with me.

I'm almost done now, and once I graduate, I can get a good management job. Business degree, bro. Companies are always hiring guys like me."

Sam sighed. "That's cool for you, man. But I already told you, that path wasn't for me."

Derrick frowned. "And where has not going to college gotten you? You're still delivering pizzas, struggling, while I'm about to start making real money."

Sam clenched his jaw. He knew Derrick wasn't trying to be a jerk, but hearing it out loud stung.

"Look, bro," Derrick continued, his tone softening, "I'm not trying to put you down. I just want to see you win. Maybe it's not too late. You could still take some classes, get a degree, turn things around."

Sam shook his head. "I don't know, man. Something about it just doesn't sit right with me."

Derrick sighed. "Then what's your plan, Sam?"

That was the question.

Sam had no answer.

All he knew was that something had to change. He couldn't keep living like this.

And in the next few days, that change would come—in the most unexpected way.

End of Chapter Two: A Crossroads

Sam is now at a critical point in his life:

- He's a single father, feeling lost and stuck.
- Derrick, about to graduate, is pushing him toward college.
- Sam is questioning everything—but still believes there's another way.

Biblical Perspective From the Author:

Life comes at us fast, and sometimes, like Sam, we find ourselves in situations we never expected. One choice, one moment, can shift the course of our lives. Sam thought he was just delivering pizzas, living in the moment, but he wasn't prepared for the responsibilities that would follow. Becoming a single father, struggling financially, and facing the pressures of life left him feeling trapped.

The Bible speaks to moments like these—when we feel lost, uncertain, and burdened by our choices. **Proverbs 16:9 (KJV)** reminds us, *"A man's heart deviseth his way: but the Lord directeth his steps."* Sam never planned for this life, but even in his mistakes and struggles, God still had a path for him.

When Derrick challenged Sam to go to college, Sam wrestled with the pressure to follow the traditional route. Many people today feel the same—pushed into a system that doesn't align with their purpose. But success isn't about following the crowd; it's about walking in wisdom. **James 1:5 (KJV)** says, *"If any of you lack wisdom, let him ask of God, that giveth to all men liberally, and upbraideth not; and it shall be given him."*

Sam didn't know the answer yet, but his story was far from over. In moments of uncertainty, we must trust that God can still lead us to the right opportunities. Mistakes don't define our future—God's guidance does.

Chapter 2 Notes

- What stood out to you in this chapter?
- How can you apply these principles to your own life?
- What action steps will you take moving forward?

Chapter 3

The Invitation

It was another long shift, another stack of pizzas in the passenger seat, another night of navigating the same streets he'd driven a hundred times before.

Sam had gotten used to it—the routine, the low pay, the feeling of just getting by. But tonight, something different was about to happen.

His last stop of the night was a backyard get together in a quiet, middle-class neighborhood. The kind of place where people had driveways, well-kept lawns, and a little extra cash to throw around.

He pulled up to the house, grabbed the five stacked pizza boxes, and made his way toward the backyard, where a group of loud, easygoing men were gathered. Laughter echoed through the yard, and for a second, Sam wished he were there to enjoy the night instead of just making a delivery.

A tall man with a confident stance and a friendly face stepped forward to greet him. "Hey, you must be the pizza guy. What's the damage?"

Sam glanced at the receipt. "Sixty-six bucks."

The man—Michael, as Sam would soon learn—pulled out his wallet, flipping through his cash.

"Man, I only got eighty on me," Michael said, holding out the bills.

Sam reached into his pocket. "I got change."

But Michael shook his head, waving him off. "Nah, keep it, buddy. That's for you."

Sam blinked. "You sure?"

Michael grinned. "Trust me. You work hard. Enjoy it."

It wasn't every day someone handed Sam a $14 tip without thinking twice. He nodded in thanks, tucking the cash into his pocket. Just as he turned to leave, Michael called out again.

"Hey, man, it's late. You got any more deliveries?"

"Nope. That was my last one."

"Well, then, why don't you grab a slice and kick back for a bit? No rush, just some good people and good food."

Sam hesitated. He wasn't the type to hang around strangers. But something in him told him to stay.

So, for the first time in a long time, Sam said yes to something unexpected.

The Conversation That Changed Everything

At first, the conversation was just small talk. The guys cracked jokes, talked about sports, and shared stories from their week.

But then, the conversation shifted.

One of the men leaned back in his chair, taking a sip of his drink. "Man, I cleared two grand this week. Not bad for a guy who makes his own schedule."

Another laughed. "Two grand? I hit twenty-two hundred. You have to step up your game, man."

Sam stopped mid-bite. Did he hear that right?

"You guys make that much?" he asked, trying not to sound too shocked.

Michael smirked. "What, you thought cab drivers were broke?"

Sam scratched his head. "I mean, yeah. I never thought you guys made that much."

Michael leaned in, eyes sharp. "You know what that means, right? If we're pulling that weekly, that's over a hundred grand a year."

Sam couldn't hide his surprise. He was barely making $600 a week after tips and taxes, and here these guys were, talking about making six figures driving cabs.

Michael must have noticed the gears turning in Sam's head because he chuckled. "And it's not just about the money, bro. It's about freedom."

"What do you mean?"

"We set our own hours, decide when we work, and still make a great living. No boss breathing down our necks. No office politics. Just the road, the passengers, and the money."

Sam had never considered anything like that before. He had spent so much time trying to figure out the "right" career that he never thought about something as simple as controlling his own time.

But then, Michael took it a step further.

"You think that's the best part?" Michael said, nodding to the other guys. "We don't just drive cabs. We invest our money together in real estate to make real money."

Sam narrowed his eyes. "What do you mean?"

One of the men, an older guy with graying hair, grinned. "I bought my first rental property five years ago with my cab earnings. Now, I own four houses, all rented out. My cab money paid for those houses."

Another man chimed in. "Yeah, and I just put a down payment on a gas station last year. It's about playing smart with the money you make."

Sam was floored. Not only were these guys making good money, but they were flipping it into something bigger.

Michael leaned back, arms crossed. "You don't need a degree. You don't need connections. You just need a car, a GPS, and the mindset to think bigger."

Sam felt something shift inside him.

All his life, he had been told that success came one way—college, job, climb the ladder, retire. But here were a bunch of regular guys, laughing, eating, and living life on their own terms.

And for the first time, Sam realized he had options.

A New Path

As the night wrapped up, Michael patted Sam on the back. "Come here next week at 6pm man. We do this all the time. Good food, good talks, and, hey, maybe by then, you'll be driving a cab too."

Sam chuckled. "Maybe."

But deep down, he knew something had changed.

That night, as he drove home, his mind was racing.

For years, he had been waiting for an opportunity to find him.

Maybe this was it.

End of Chapter Three: A New Perspective

Now, Sam is standing at the edge of a decision that could change his life.

- He has met Michael, his second mentor, and a group of successful, independent cab drivers.
- He's realizing that freedom is just as important as money.
- He sees that wealth isn't just about earning—it's about what you do with what you earn.

Biblical Perspective From the Author: The Value of Seeking Wisdom

Sam's introduction to Michael and the group of cab drivers was more than just luck—it was a clear example of Proverbs 4:7 (KJV): *"Wisdom is the principal thing; therefore get wisdom: and with all thy getting get understanding."*

Many people overlook opportunities because they dismiss wisdom that comes from unconventional sources. Sam could have ignored the knowledge of these cab drivers, assuming that wealth only came through traditional paths like college and corporate jobs. Instead, he humbled himself and listened, much like Solomon, who asked God for wisdom rather than riches (1 Kings 3:9-12).

The Bible repeatedly emphasizes that wealth and success are often the result of applied wisdom, discipline, and understanding. In the parable of the talents (Matthew 25:14-30), those who used what they were given wisely were rewarded with more. Sam's willingness to learn from experienced individuals positioned him to grow financially.

True wisdom isn't just about acquiring knowledge—it's about applying it effectively. The right opportunities and financial breakthroughs come when we seek and apply godly wisdom in our decision-making.

Chapter 3 Notes

- What stood out to you in this chapter?
- How can you apply these principles to your own life?
- What action steps will you take moving forward?

Chapter 4

The Blueprint for Freedom

All week, Sam couldn't shake what Michael had told him. It played over and over in his mind—how these cab drivers weren't just making money, but controlling their time, investing, building real wealth. It was the kind of conversation he had never had before, and now that the door was cracked open, he wanted to push it wide.

By the time Saturday rolled around, he wasn't just eager—he was restless. The weekly gathering was set for six, but at five o'clock sharp, Sam was standing on Michael's porch, ringing the doorbell.

When Michael opened the door, he smirked, shaking his head. "Man, I knew you'd show up early."

Sam laughed. "Yeah, I couldn't wait, man. I just… I needed to hear more. Everything you told me last week, I've been thinking about it nonstop."

Michael stepped aside, waving him in. "Come on in, then. I already know what this is about."

They settled into the living room, and Michael leaned back, studying him. "I can see it in your face—you're at that point where you know there's more, but you don't know how to get it."

Sam nodded. "Yeah, exactly. I feel like I've been stuck just… surviving. Working, paying bills, repeating the same cycle every week. It's like I've been asleep, and last week, you woke me up."

Michael smiled. "Yeah, I know that feeling. I was just like you when I was younger—confused, looking around, wondering if I was making the right decisions while everybody told me college was the only way. Told me that if I didn't go, I'd regret it." He shook his head. "Man, let me tell you something. The biggest regret a man can have is not fighting for his freedom."

That word hit Sam differently.

Michael leaned forward. "If you don't have your own freedom, then jobs, people, and bills will dictate what you do, where you go, and how you live. That's not a life—that's a cage."

Sam let that sink in.

Michael continued, his voice steady. "I got multi-unit properties. I've got investments. I've helped start businesses that still pay me passive income to this day. That means money coming in whether I work or not."

Sam's eyebrows raised. "Passive income?"

Michael nodded. "Yeah. Money that doesn't need me to clock in or show up somewhere to earn it. That's the key, Sam. You want to get to a point where you're making money while you sleep."

Sam was listening closely now. "But I have to ask you something, man. If you've got all that, why are you still driving a cab?"

Michael grinned. "Good question. Let me tell you why." He leaned back, stretching his arms. "I love meeting people. Some of the best business connections I've ever made? Came right through my cab. Investors, CEOs, people with money and knowledge I never would've had access to if I wasn't driving around this city. You'd be surprised who gets into the backseat of a cab."

Sam nodded slowly.

"And besides, I enjoy it. Some people play ball on the weekends, some people gamble, some people play video games. Me? I drive. It's my way of staying connected, keeping my energy up, and expanding my network."

Sam had never thought of a job like that before—as something you do because you want to, not because you have to.

Michael smirked. "Let me guess—you're ready to start driving, huh?"

Sam chuckled. "Man, more than that. I want to know everything you know. I don't just want to make money—I want to make moves."

Michael sat up. "Alright, then. If you're serious, I'm going to set you up for success. But I need you to listen and do exactly what I tell you."

Sam nodded. "I'm listening."

Michael laid it out.

"I own a four-unit apartment building, and I got a unit sitting empty. Here's what I'm going to do for you. I'll let you stay there rent-free for six months. No bills, no expenses. But every dollar you would have spent on rent? You're going to put that in a seed fund—an account strictly for your first real estate investment."

Sam's eyes widened. He had never heard of anything like that before.

Michael wasn't done. "You need to establish credit the right way. Go to the bank and take out a $1,000 loan, but secure it with your own $1,000 in savings. That way, the bank sees you as a low risk. Pay that off in six months, and boom—your credit score jumps."

Sam was locked in.

Michael leaned forward. "Next, get yourself a secured credit card with a $500 limit. Use it only for gas, and never spend more than 30% of the limit. Pay it off in full every month. Do that for six months, and you'll have solid credit."

Sam was already mapping it out in his head.

"And, of course, start driving a cab. You're already on the road delivering pizzas—you might as well make real money while you're at it."

Sam took a deep breath. This wasn't just some conversation anymore. This was a plan.

Michael slapped his shoulder. "I can't give you everything, Sam. But I can give you the knowledge. The rest? That's on you."

Sam nodded. "I got this."

Michael smiled. "We'll see."

The First Steps Toward Freedom

The next morning, Sam wasted no time.

- He moved into Michael's unit, stacking every saved dollar into his **seed fund.**
- He went to the bank, took out the secured **$1,000 loan**, and started making his payments.
- He got the secured credit card, following Michael's instructions to the letter.
- And by the end of the week, he had signed up to **drive a cab.**

For the first time in his life, he wasn't just working—he was building.

And he wasn't looking back.

End of Chapter Four: A New Beginning

Sam is finally making moves, setting himself up for financial freedom.

- He has a rent-free place to save money.
- He is building credit the right way.
- He is making more money driving cabs than he ever did delivering pizza.

- He has a new group of mentors pushing him toward wealth.

Biblical Perspective From the Author: The Power of Diligence and Opportunity

At this stage in Sam's journey, he hasn't yet made his first investment, but he is laying the groundwork. The Bible speaks to the importance of preparation, discipline, and stewardship. Proverbs 21:5 (KJV) states, *"The thoughts of the diligent tend only to plenteousness; but of every one that is hasty only to want."* This highlights the necessity of planning and consistency. Sam is beginning to make intentional moves—saving money, building credit, and surrounding himself with mentors. These small but critical steps are positioning him for long-term success.

Luke 16:10 (KJV) also reinforces this principle: *"He that is faithful in that which is least is faithful also in much: and he that is unjust in the least is unjust also in much."* Sam is learning to be faithful with the small steps before he handles greater responsibilities. He doesn't jump into wealth overnight; instead, he practices discipline and wise stewardship, which will later allow him to seize bigger opportunities.

Success isn't about rushing into investments—it's about preparing wisely, making strategic decisions, and being patient for the right opportunities. When you are faithful over the small things, God will entrust you with more. Sam is walking this principle out, unknowingly setting himself up for financial freedom.

Chapter 4 Notes

- What stood out to you in this chapter?
- How can you apply these principles to your own life?
- What action steps will you take moving forward?

Chapter 5

The First Big Deal

Sam had been driving cabs for over a year now, following every piece of advice Michael had given him. One of the biggest things Michael had drilled into his head was **patience**—the right opportunity would come, but he had to be ready when it did.

Over that year, Sam had seen a few deals come and go—some promising, some just not quite right. He had gone to property showings, run the numbers, even made offers, but nothing had materialized. Still, he stuck with the plan, knowing that the right deal would present itself when the time was right.

Then, on an otherwise normal day, it happened.

A Chance Encounter

Sam had picked up a middle-aged man from a quiet residential neighborhood. The man looked tired, like he had a lot on his mind. As they drove through the city, casual conversation turned into something much more valuable.

"I'm actually on my way to meet with my real estate agent," the man said, looking out the window.

"Oh yeah? Buying something new?" Sam asked, keeping his eyes on the road.

The man let out a small chuckle. "Nah, actually selling. I own a three-unit building, but I'm relocating and don’t want to manage it anymore. Figured it’s time to let it go."

Sam’s ears perked up. Three units? A rental property?

"Really? You got someone lined up to buy it yet?" Sam asked, keeping his tone as casual as possible.

"Not yet. My agent’s just starting to put it on the market," the man replied. Then he glanced over. "Why, you know somebody looking?"

Sam didn’t hesitate. “Yeah. Maybe me.”

The man raised an eyebrow, but he didn’t laugh. Instead, he nodded. "Alright then. Tell you what—I'll give you my number. If you're serious, let’s talk."

As soon as the ride was over, Sam saved the number in his phone and immediately drove over to Michael’s house.

Michael’s Approval

Michael listened as Sam laid everything out.

“Three-unit building, decent neighborhood, and he’s looking to sell fast,” Sam said, his excitement barely contained. “What do you think?”

Michael leaned back in his chair, nodding slowly. “Sounds like a solid opportunity. But let me ask you something—do you think you can pull off this deal?”

Sam exhaled. “I don’t have the full down payment yet, but the seller let me put $10,000 on contract to close this deal in 60 days. I was thinking… maybe I could structure something creative?"

Michael grinned. "Now you're thinking like an investor."

They ran the numbers together. The seller was asking $675,000 for the property. It was a three-unit apartment building, each unit being a two-bedroom renting for $2,000 per month.

"It's decent," Michael said. "But before you do anything more, you need to know the real value of this building. Get an appraisal."

The next day, Sam arranged for an appraisal, and the results came back in a few weeks: $710,000—higher than what the seller was asking.

Michael smiled when he saw the numbers. "This is good. This means you already have $35,000 in equity the moment you buy it, plus it's very little to improve. Now, how's the financing looking?"

Structuring the Deal

Sam went to the bank, armed with the appraisal and his financial records. Because of the credit moves he had made over the past year—paying off his secured loan, maintaining his credit card the right way, and building his savings—the bank approved him for a loan.

The bank agreed to finance 80% of the appraised value—which meant they would give him $568,000.

That still left $107,000 to cover.

That's when Sam got creative.

He called the seller and set up a meeting. When they sat down, Sam laid out his offer:

- The bank would cover $568,000 of the purchase price.
- Instead of coming up with the remaining balance in cash, the seller would finance the rest.
- Sam would pay the remaining $97,000 over seven years at 6% interest.

The seller thought about it. He wasn't in a rush for cash—he just wanted to offload the property without the hassle of waiting for the right buyer.

After some negotiation, he agreed.

Sam was now the owner of a three-unit apartment building—only spending $10,000 out of his pocket.

Making It Profitable

At first, Sam was making just enough to cover his expenses. The property was paying for itself, but the real wealth would come from cash flow.

So, he did what any smart investor would do—he made minor improvements.

He fixed up the units, added small upgrades, and increased the rent from $2,000 to $2,240 per unit.

Now, instead of just breaking even, he was cash-flowing $645 every single month.

For the first time, Sam wasn't just working for money—money was working for him.

A New Life Begins

Sam stood outside his newly purchased building one evening, watching the sun set behind the city skyline.

A year ago, he was delivering pizzas, wondering how he was going to take care of his son, struggling to make ends meet.

Now, he was a property owner.

And he had done it without following the traditional path everyone had told him was the only way.

Michael had been right all along—freedom wasn't given, it was taken.

This was just the beginning.

End of Chapter Five

Sam is now on his way, having successfully acquired his first property using creative financing and mentorship. In the next chapter, Sam continues growing his portfolio, setting himself up for even greater financial freedom.

Biblical Perspective From the Author: Wisdom in Financial Decisions

Sam's ability to recognize opportunities and take strategic action aligns with biblical principles of wisdom and stewardship. **Proverbs 24:3-4 (KJV)** states:

"Through wisdom is an house builded; and by understanding it is established: And by knowledge shall the chambers be filled with all precious and pleasant riches."

This scripture emphasizes that success is not just about money—it requires wisdom, understanding, and knowledge. Sam didn't blindly jump into a deal; he sought mentorship, carefully analyzed the numbers, and structured the financing creatively to make his first property work for him.

Additionally, **Luke 14:28 (KJV)** reminds us:

"For which of you, intending to build a tower, sitteth not down first, and counteth the cost, whether he have sufficient to finish it?"

Sam applied this principle by making sure the deal made financial sense before committing. He took the time to get the property appraised, secure bank financing, and negotiate terms with the seller, ensuring that his first investment would be profitable rather than a burden.

This chapter teaches that wealth-building isn't about taking reckless risks—it's about using wisdom, seeking wise counsel, and structuring deals in a way that allows you to grow while minimizing unnecessary financial strain. When you apply biblical wisdom to your financial choices, you set yourself up for long-term success.

Chapter 5 Notes

- What stood out to you in this chapter?
- How can you apply these principles to your own life?
- What action steps will you take moving forward?

Chapter 6

The Power of Association

Sam had spent the last year learning the ropes of being a landlord—handling tenant issues, making property improvements, understanding tax benefits, and dealing with unexpected challenges. It wasn't easy, but it was preparing him for something bigger.

One of the biggest lessons Michael had taught him was that being around like-minded people creates opportunities. And that's exactly how Sam's next deal came to him.

An Opportunity in the Group

The cab drivers had always been a tight-knit group, and while most of them loved to brag about their weekly earnings, there was one guy who kept to himself—Jack.

Jack was an older driver, not flashy like the rest, but everyone knew he had been in the game for a long time. One Saturday night at their usual gathering, Jack casually mentioned something that made Sam's ears perk up.

"I'm thinking about selling one of my buildings," Jack said, sipping his drink. "Been holding on to it for years, but I'm ready to cash out."

The group nodded, but no one jumped at the offer. They were all comfortable where they were, but Sam was still building.

"How much are you asking?" Sam asked.

Jack looked at him. "$800,000. But I'd be willing to work something out with the right person."

Sam sat up. He was ready for his second property.

Negotiating the Deal

Sam knew how to negotiate now. He wasn't desperate, and he had learned how to structure a deal that worked in his favor.

After a few conversations, Jack agreed to drop the price to $780,000—he wasn't in a rush, and he wanted the property to go to someone who would take care of it.

This wasn't just another rental building. It was a four-unit apartment complex with a commercial storefront on the ground floor.

Here was the rental breakdown:

- **Third Floor:** 3-bedroom apartment - **$2,100/month**
- **Second Floor:** 2-bedroom apartment - **$1,700/month**
- **Second Floor:** 1-bedroom apartment - **$1,500/month**
- **Ground Floor:** Commercial storefront - **$2,500/month**
- **Behind the storefront:** Small 1-bedroom unit - **$1,000/month**

Total rental income: $8,800 per month.

That wasn't bad, but Sam immediately saw potential.

By making improvements and adjusting rents to reflect market value, he could push the income up to $10,700 per month.

Sam Signed a sale agreement and based his purchase on the appraisal coming in over $100,000 than his agreed purchase price.

When the results came back, he couldn't believe it—the property was valued at $1,000,000.

That meant before he even closed, he had $220,000 in instant equity.

How Sam Structured the Purchase

Because of the strong cash flow and property value, the bank agreed to loan Sam 80% of the appraised value, meaning they gave him $800,000, even though he had negotiated the purchase price at $780,000.

At closing, Sam walked away with $20,000 in his pocket.

Michael had always told him, "It's not just about owning property—it's about structuring deals that make sense."

New Cash Flow, New Lifestyle

After making strategic improvements, Sam successfully increased the total rent to $11,000 per month.

His monthly mortgage payment on the $800,000 loan at 6% over 20 years came out to $5,731.45 per month.

After factoring in estimated expenses of $3,300 per month, his net cash flow from this property was $1,968.55 per month.

When adding in the $645 cash flow from his first property, Sam was now making $2,613.55 per month in passive income.

This wasn't from clocking in somewhere. This was money coming in every month whether he worked or not.

A Different Kind of Freedom

Sam stood outside his new building one evening, looking up at the windows, the storefront, the life he was creating.

Just a few years ago, he had been delivering pizzas, struggling to make ends meet. Now, he owned two properties, had hundreds of thousands in equity, and was making more every month from his investments than most people made at a full-time job.

And the crazy part? He was just getting started.

End of Chapter Six

Now, Sam is two properties deep, generating over $2,600 per month in passive income, and walking into his next level of financial freedom.

In the next chapter, he will make one more investment before reconnecting with Derrick.

Biblical Perspective From the Author: The Rewards of Diligence and Faithful Stewardship

As Sam continues to expand his real estate portfolio, his journey reflects the biblical principle of diligence and faithful stewardship. Proverbs 13:4 (KJV) states: *"The soul of the sluggard desireth, and hath nothing: but the soul of the diligent shall be made fat."*

Sam's success wasn't instantaneous—he had to manage his properties, deal with tenants, and learn through experience. His persistence and commitment to managing his resources wisely mirror the diligence that Scripture encourages.

Additionally, Luke 16:10 (KJV) reminds us: *"He that is faithful in that which is least is faithful also in much: and he that is unjust in the least is unjust also in much."* Sam proved himself faithful with his first property, handling responsibilities well, which positioned him for larger opportunities.

This chapter teaches that financial growth is a process, requiring patience, discipline, and a commitment to faithful stewardship. When we prove responsible with small blessings, God entrusts us with greater ones.

Chapter 6 Notes

- What stood out to you in this chapter?
- How can you apply these principles to your own life?
- What action steps will you take moving forward?

Chapter 7

The Big Flip

For the first time in his life, Sam wasn't just getting by—he was thriving. His monthly cash flow was approaching $3,000, and his net worth had exceeded $300,000. The appreciation of his first property, combined with the equity in his second, meant that if he sold everything today, he'd walk away with a life-changing amount of cash. But Sam had no interest in cashing out. He was just getting started.

It was a typical day when Sam ran into his neighbor, Mr. Langley. They often made small talk, but today's conversation took a turn that piqued Sam's interest. Langley mentioned that his elderly mother was moving out of her home after forty years. She couldn't maintain it anymore, and her children lived too far away to help. They had decided to sell the house and move her in with family. Sam was curious and asked what they were looking to get for it. Langley explained that they hoped to sell it for around $550,000, but they knew it needed work to reach that value.

Sam saw an opportunity. "What if I could pay you cash and close in thirty days?" he asked. Langley raised an eyebrow. "Cash?" Sam nodded, keeping his tone casual. "I'd take it as-is. No agent fees, no waiting for buyers. But to make it work, I'd need a better price." After some negotiation, they settled on $360,000. Sam now had a deal in hand, but there was just one issue—he didn't have $360,000 in cash.

That Saturday, at the group's weekly meeting, Sam pitched the opportunity to Michael and the other investors. "This isn't our usual multi-unit deal," he admitted, "but the numbers make sense. This house is worth between $650,000 and $700,000 after some renovations. If we flip it, there's six figures of profit on the table." Michael leaned back in his chair, rubbing his chin. "How much work are we talking?"

"Not much," Sam said. "It's outdated but structurally solid. A full remodel—floors, kitchens, bathrooms, paint. Maybe $90,000 to $100,000."

Before Michael could respond, Paul—one of the investors—spoke up. "I don't know, man," Paul said, crossing his arms. "Single-family flips aren't our thing. And if the market shifts, we could be stuck with it."

Sam was ready for this. "That's why I ran comps," he said. "Houses in worse condition are selling for $600,000. With the upgrades, this one could go for $700,000 easy."

Paul frowned, thinking. The room was quiet for a moment before one of the other investors, Mark, spoke up. "I'm in. If we can make six figures, I'm good with it."

Michael smirked and turned to Paul. "Paul?"

Paul hesitated, then sighed. "Fine. I'm in too."

With that, the deal was set. The investors pooled together $350,000, and Sam added his $10,000 deposit. The contract was signed, and within two weeks, the seller was out, and Sam took possession of the property.

Once the property was secured, Sam needed to maximize the profits by modernizing the house to get top market value. He went back to Michael and suggested bringing in one more investor for $100,000 to cover renovations. This final investor agreed, and Sam was now in at $460,000

Renovations started fast, and at first, everything went smoothly. Sam hired contractors, set a 60-day timeline, and got to work. Then, problems started arising. The city took longer than expected to approve electrical permits, causing a two-week delay. Once demolition started, they discovered hidden water damage in the walls, which forced them to add an extra $5,000 to the renovation budget. A subcontractor for the plumbing work walked off the job after an argument over scheduling, leaving Sam scrambling to find a replacement.

One evening, Sam vented his frustration to Michael, who listened and then simply smiled. "Welcome to real estate," Michael said with a chuckle. "You're doing everything right, but deals never go perfectly. What matters is how you push through."

Sam took Michael's advice, focused on problem-solving instead of panicking, and by the end of 60 days, the house was fully renovated and modernized.

With all the work completed, Sam listed the home at $750,000. For three weeks, there was little movement—some showings, but no serious buyers. Doubt began to creep in, but Michael assured him that patience was key. Finally, after almost a month, a buyer submitted an offer at $730,000. It wasn't the full asking price, but it was close enough, and Sam accepted.

After closing, he repaid each investor their original amount plus 10%:

Investor 1 (Mark): $100,000 → $110,000

Investor 2 (Paul): $100,000 → $110,000

Investor 3 (Michael): $150,000 → $165,000

Renovation Investor: $100,000 → $110,000

Total Repayment: $495,000

When the dust settled, Sam walked away with a $224,000 profit.

Sam sat in his car, staring at the check in his hand. Just a few years ago, he had been delivering pizzas, struggling to support his son. Now, he was flipping houses, collecting rent, and watching his wealth grow. This wasn't luck. This was strategy, mentorship, and execution.

And he wasn't stopping here.

Key Takeaways from Chapter Seven

- **Sam completed his first house flip and made $224,000.** He structured the deal with private investors and didn't use his own money beyond the deposit.
- **Investors were skeptical, but the numbers made sense.** Paul had concerns, but once he saw the **comparable market values**, he agreed.
- **Obstacles appeared, but Sam learned how to push through.** Permit delays, **unexpected repair costs**, and **contractor issues** tested him, but he **found solutions instead of panicking**.
- **Sam's cash flow and net worth are growing.** His **cash flow is close to $3,000 per month**, and with this deal, his **total wealth has jumped significantly**.
- **This success fuels his next moves.** Sam now has the experience, confidence, and financial backing to **scale his investments further**.

Biblical Perspective From the Author: Patience, Strategy, and Trusting God's Timing

Sam's journey in this chapter reflects a key biblical principle: success often comes through patience, perseverance, and faith in God's timing. While his deal was structured well, it didn't come without setbacks—permit delays, unexpected repair costs, and contractor issues. Yet, he stayed the course, trusting that his preparation and diligence would lead to success.

Galatians 6:9 (KJV) states: *"And let us not be weary in well doing: for in due season we shall reap, if we faint not."*

This verse reminds us that challenges are part of the process, but we must not give up. Just like Sam pressed forward despite obstacles, we, too, must keep going when things don't go as planned, knowing that our faithfulness will bear fruit in due time.

Additionally, **Proverbs 16:3 (KJV)** provides wisdom on the role of commitment and faith in our endeavors: *"Commit thy works unto the Lord, and thy thoughts shall be established."*

Sam's success was not just about making money—it was about learning, growing, and applying wisdom at every turn. He sought mentorship, structured deals carefully, and remained patient when things seemed uncertain. The lesson here is clear: when we commit our plans to God, act with wisdom, and trust His timing, He will guide us toward victory—even when the journey is filled with challenges.

Chapter 7 Notes

- What stood out to you in this chapter?
- How can you apply these principles to your own life?
- What action steps will you take moving forward?

Chapter 8

Breaking into Commercial Real Estate

At just 24 years old, Sam had already achieved what most people spent a lifetime chasing. His net worth had surpassed $500,000, a combination of rental properties, equity appreciation, and his recent six-figure payday from the house flip. He was generating nearly $3,000 a month in passive income, and for the first time, he truly believed in his own financial future.

It wasn't luck that had gotten him here. It was the mentorship he had received, the decisions he had made, and the opportunities he had seized.

Tony, the pizza shop owner, had planted the first seed—the idea that financial success wasn't tied to a college degree. Then Michael had come into his life, guiding him on real estate, leverage, and wealth-building strategies. Now, Sam was actively seeking his next big move, no longer waiting for success to find him.

A Chance Encounter with a Game-Changer

One evening, while driving his cab, Sam picked up a well-dressed man outside an upscale restaurant. The man was on a date, but when his date stepped away to take a phone call, Sam struck up a conversation.

"You look like you just closed a deal," Sam said, half-joking.

The man chuckled. "Something like that. I'm a real estate agent—commercial properties, mostly apartments and mixed-use buildings."

That got Sam's attention. "I've been in the game for a few years," Sam said. "I've got a couple of multi-units under my belt. I'm always looking for the next opportunity."

The agent looked intrigued. "Most guys driving cabs aren't in real estate."

Sam smirked. "Most guys don't know how to use their money the right way."

The agent nodded approvingly. "I like that. You never know who has the bag. Some of my best deals have come from people no one expects to be serious investors."

They exchanged numbers, and Sam told him, "If you come across any solid multi-family deals, I want first dibs before they hit the market."

The agent smiled. "That's exactly the kind of buyer I like working with."

The Deal That Changed Everything

Six months later, Sam got a call from the agent.

"I've got something interesting for you. A seller is looking to unload three properties as a package deal. He wants a single buyer to take everything at once if possible. Would you be interested?"

Sam hesitated. Three properties? That was a huge leap from what he was used to. But he remembered Michael's words:

"Never judge a deal before fully exploring it. The first offer is just a starting point."

"Tell me more," Sam said.

The agent explained that the seller was a wealthy investor who had just been diagnosed with aggressive cancer. He wanted to liquidate his assets, settle his affairs, and enjoy whatever time he had left.

Sam agreed to meet and tour the properties.

The most attractive asset in the package was a commercial building with two storefronts and eight one-bedroom apartments. The seller originally listed the property for $1,000,000, but Sam knew from experience that asking prices were just that—asking prices.

Financing Struggles and Hard Lessons

Sam immediately saw the potential in the deal, but there was a problem: the seller wanted cash. He wasn't willing to hold a note because he didn't know how much time he had left. This meant Sam needed to put more of his money in upfront.

Sam had over $200,000 in cash, so he was confident about getting a standard 20% down commercial loan. But he quickly ran into trouble.

The first ten banks he approached turned him down.

One bank told him he lacked experience with commercial properties.

Another said his tax returns didn't show enough income.

One simply said, "We don't finance deals this size for first-time commercial buyers with units this big."

Sam had done everything right, built his portfolio, maintained good credit, and yet, these banks were shutting the door on him. It was frustrating, but Sam kept his faith and continued to pray daily about the right doors opening up.

The seller, however, saw that Sam was serious and agreed to extend the closing by 60 days—but with a condition.

"If you can't close in 60 days, you lose your $10,000 deposit," the seller warned. "I'll find another buyer."

Sam took the risk.

Turning Rejection into Negotiation Power

Sam went back to the seller and played his hand.

"I've been having issues with financing because the bank doesn't see this property as worth a million," Sam told him. "I still want to buy it, but I need you to be flexible."

The seller listened carefully. He didn't want to lose time, so he dropped the price to $905,000.

That single move saved Sam nearly $100,000 before he even closed.

Finding the Right Bank

After weeks of frustration, Sam finally met with a small local bank that actually took the time to go through his portfolio.

"We like what you're doing," the loan officer said. "We're willing to finance 80% of the deal, which comes out to $724,000."

Sam put down $181,000 in cash and finally closed on the property.

Unlocking the Property's True Potential

When Sam took over, the eight apartments were renting for $900/month each, and the two storefronts were paying $1,500/month each.

That wasn't bad, but Sam knew they were underpriced.

Over the next two years, he upgraded the apartments, refreshed the exterior, and marketed to better tenants.

By the end of that period, the apartments were renting for $1,250/month, and the storefronts had increased to $2,000/month each.

Because of the higher rental income, the building was now worth $1.6 million.

At 26 years old, Sam had doubled the property's value and positioned himself as a serious player in the commercial real estate game.

Breaking Down the Numbers

- Purchase Price: $905,000
- Bank Loan (80%): $724,000
- Sam's Down Payment: $181,000
- Original Monthly Rental Income:
    - Apartments: $7,200 ($900 × 8)
    - Storefronts: $3,000 ($1,500 × 2)
    - Total: $10,200/month
- New Monthly Rental Income (After Improvements):
    - Apartments: $10,000 ($1,250 × 8)
    - Storefronts: $4,000 ($2,000 × 2)
    - Total: $14,000/month
- New Building Value: $1.6 million
- Sam's Equity Increase: $696,000 in 3 years

A Growing Empire

Sam looked back on the past few years and realized how far he had come. From delivering pizzas to owning millions in real estate, he had made every decision count.

But he wasn't done yet.

This was only the beginning.

End of Chapter Eight

Sam is now 26 years old, owns a high-value commercial property, and has dramatically increased his wealth and cash flow.

Sam looked back on the past few years and realized how far he had come. Just seven years out of high school, he had gone from delivering pizzas to owning over a million dollars in real estate equity and generating nearly $12,000 a month in passive income. What had once seemed impossible was now his reality.

The numbers didn't lie. With $696,000 in equity from his latest commercial property and another $350,000 from his previous buildings, Sam's total net worth had officially surpassed $1,046,000. He was now a millionaire—a title that once felt reserved for people born into wealth or given lucky breaks. But he had built it from nothing.

His real estate portfolio was now bringing in $11,800 per month in cash flow. The new commercial building alone generated $8,800 monthly, after covering the $4,200 mortgage and $1,000 in expenses, while his previous properties added another $3,000 in cash flow.

This wasn't luck. It wasn't just ambition. It was strategy, patience, and execution.

And he wasn't stopping here.

Biblical Perspective From the Author: Faith, Favor, and Strategic Action

Sam's journey into commercial real estate illustrates the power of perseverance, negotiation, and divine favor. Despite facing multiple rejections, he didn't let discouragement stop him. He persisted, adapted his strategy, and ultimately secured a deal that would change his financial trajectory.

This aligns with **Isaiah 41:10 (KJV):** *"Fear thou not; for I am with thee: be not dismayed; for I am thy God: I will strengthen thee; yea, I will help thee; yea, I will uphold thee with the right hand of my righteousness."*

Sam could have easily let fear stop him when the banks kept rejecting him. Instead, he kept pushing forward, trusting that the right opportunity would come. This scripture reminds us that when God has a plan for us, we must trust that He will uphold us through every challenge.

Additionally, **Psalm 1:3 (KJV)** states: *"And he shall be like a tree planted by the rivers of water, that bringeth forth his fruit in his season; his leaf also shall not wither; and whatsoever he doeth shall prosper."*

Sam positioned himself in the right places, surrounding himself with mentors, wise counsel, and opportunities. Like a tree planted by the water, he remained rooted in his vision, and in due time, he saw his investments prosper. This verse encourages us to stay planted in the right environments so that God's favor can bring increase.

Lastly, **2 Chronicles 15:7 (KJV)** declares: *"Be ye strong therefore, and let not your hands be weak: for your work shall be rewarded."*

Sam worked tirelessly, faced setbacks, and encountered obstacles, yet he remained **resilient.** This scripture reinforces the idea that diligence and faith lead to rewards—whether in business, personal growth, or financial breakthroughs.

When we combine faith, persistence, and wisdom, doors will open, and God will order our steps into financial freedom and generational wealth.

Chapter 8 Notes

- What stood out to you in this chapter?
- How can you apply these principles to your own life?
- What action steps will you take moving forward?

Chapter 9

The Power of Sharing Knowledge

Sam had built a life that most people only dreamed about, yet he wasn't done. He had total financial freedom, yet he still enjoyed driving his cab. Just like Michael and the rest of the guys in the group, he saw it not as a job, but as a way to connect with people, hear stories, and sometimes, find new opportunities.

At 26 years old, he could have retired, but he wasn't looking to stop working—he was looking to stop struggling. With nearly $12,000 in monthly cash flow from his properties, he didn't need to drive for money, but it was an extra $1,500 a week that gave him complete financial control. He owned his own home now, a place he purchased without touching his earned income—his investments covered the mortgage.

His entire lifestyle was funded by his assets. And yet, one unexpected encounter would show him that he was sitting on another fortune, one he hadn't even considered.

A Passenger Who Changed Everything

One evening, after dropping off a fare, Sam picked up a middle-aged man carrying a small briefcase. The man slid into the backseat, adjusting his coat as Sam pulled off.

"Long day?" Sam asked casually.

"Always," the man said with a chuckle. "I write books, so my schedule is all over the place."

That caught Sam's attention. "Books? What kind?"

"Mostly non-fiction," the man replied. "I take things I've learned in my life and share them with others—giving them practical steps to do what I've done."

Sam nodded, intrigued. "So, you basically teach people through books?"

"Exactly," the man said. "I help them see what's possible, inspire them to take action."

Sam thought about that for a moment before asking, "What's the business side of it? Do people actually make money writing books?"

The man smiled. "Let me put it this way—if you have valuable knowledge, something that can help others change their lives, and you package it into a book, it becomes an asset. It's something that makes you money, even when you're not working."

Sam was intrigued.

"Let me ask you this," the author continued, "what do you specialize in?"

"Well," Sam said, "besides driving a cab, I've built a real estate portfolio—rental properties, commercial units, investments. I've built something from nothing, just leveraging the money I had and growing it over time."

The author raised an eyebrow. "Really? Tell me about it."

Sam, proud of what he had accomplished, spent the next few minutes breaking it down—how he got started, the mentors who guided him, the creative ways he secured financing, and how he built wealth without following society's traditional path.

When he finished, the author sat back and laughed.

"You have no idea how valuable that story is," he said. "You just gave me ten years of knowledge in ten minutes. But here's the thing—you can only tell it to one person at a time. What if you wrote it in a book? What if you packaged it so that thousands—maybe even millions—could learn from your journey?"

Sam had never considered that before.

"You're sitting on another major income stream, my friend," the author continued. "If you take everything you just told me and put it into a book or course, you could create something that pays you forever."

It was at that moment that a lightbulb went off in Sam's mind.

From Idea to Execution

That single conversation stayed with Sam long after the author stepped out of his cab. He never saw the man again, but he didn't need to—he had already received the insight that would change his life again.

The following Monday, Sam sat down in his home office and started writing. He poured everything onto the page—the mistakes, the wins, the mindset shifts, and most importantly, the blueprint for how others could follow in his footsteps.

It took him two months to get the book done, working in the early mornings before he drove his cab and in the evenings before bed. He had it edited, formatted, and ready for publication.

And when the time came, he knew exactly what to call it. **"The Rich Cab Driver."**

The title was perfect because Sam knew firsthand how a simple job behind the wheel of a cab had led him to financial freedom. He wanted people to understand that the job you do isn't what determines your wealth—it's what you do with the money you make.

A New Revenue Stream Opens

When Sam published his book, he had no idea how big it would become. He marketed it online, used social media, and reached out to other entrepreneurs, investors, and cab drivers who might find his story inspiring.

Within the first six months, he had sold 100,000 copies.

At just $10 per book, that meant $1,000,000 in sales.

After covering marketing costs, printing, and distribution expenses, Sam walked away with a $500,000 profit—from just telling his story.

The Final Piece of the Puzzle

Sam had built wealth through real estate, created cash flow through rentals, and now he had added an entirely new income stream—selling knowledge.

The best part? This money required no tenants, no property management, no bank loans.

For the first time, Sam had fully leveraged his experiences to create passive income in a way that required no physical labor.

At this point, Sam wasn't just a real estate investor. He was an entrepreneur, an author, and an inspiration to thousands.

His millionaire status wasn't a dream anymore—it was his reality.

And just like every other opportunity in his life, it had started with a single cab ride.

Biblical Perspective From the Author: The Power of Wisdom and Sharing Knowledge

Sam's journey into writing and teaching others through his book reflects a powerful biblical principle—wisdom and knowledge should be shared, not hoarded. When we take what we've learned and help others, God blesses that effort and multiplies the impact.

This aligns with **Proverbs 11:25 (KJV):** *"The liberal soul shall be made fat: and he that watereth shall be watered also himself."*

Sam poured his knowledge into a book, and in return, he received abundance—not just financially, but in purpose and legacy. When we freely give and teach others, we position ourselves for even greater blessings.

Another powerful scripture that reflects Sam's journey is **Ecclesiastes 9:10 (KJV):** *"Whatsoever thy hand findeth to do, do it with thy might; for there is no work, nor device, nor knowledge, nor wisdom, in the grave, whither thou goest."*

Sam didn't just sit on his knowledge—he took action. He recognized that his experiences weren't just for him; they were meant to inspire, teach, and uplift others. This verse reminds us that our gifts and knowledge should be put to work while we have the opportunity.

Finally, **Matthew 5:16 (KJV)** declares: *"Let your light so shine before men, that they may see your good works, and glorify your Father which is in heaven."*

Sam's story became more than just personal success—it became a light for others. His testimony, his work, and his willingness to teach reflected God's principles of stewardship, faith, and perseverance.

The key takeaway from this chapter is simple: your knowledge and experiences are valuable. When you share wisdom, you create opportunities—not just for others, but for yourself.

Chapter 9 Notes

- What stood out to you in this chapter?
- How can you apply these principles to your own life?
- What action steps will you take moving forward?

Chapter 10

The Reunion

Sam had been so busy building his empire that he hadn't spoken to Derrick in years. Life had taken them in different directions, and though they had been best friends growing up, the realities of adulthood had pulled them apart.

It had been four years since Derrick graduated from college, and during that time, he had faced his own set of challenges. Armed with a business administration degree and another 2 year degree in finance, he had been eager to land a management job right out of school, believing that his first degree alone would guarantee him a high-paying career.

But reality had hit him hard.

Derrick had struggled to find stable employment. His expectations of landing a $100,000+ corporate position had quickly been crushed when he realized that thousands of other graduates had the same degree, competing for the same limited positions.

His first job? A manager at a fast-food seafood chain, making $40,000 a year.

Not exactly the dream job he had envisioned after four years of college.

Still, he stayed there for two years, gaining experience but feeling unfulfilled. Eventually, he landed a slightly better job at a communications company, managing a small staff for $55,000 a year. It was an improvement, but even after taxes, he was barely making more than $1,000 a week.

Derrick felt trapped.

The long hours, limited opportunities for advancement, and financial struggles were weighing on him.

To make matters worse, he was now engaged, and while he wanted to buy a home and build a future with his fiancée, his salary wasn't enough to afford the lifestyle he had always dreamed of.

It was in the midst of these frustrations that he thought about Sam.

He had heard bits and pieces about how Sam had been doing well, but the last time they had spoken, Sam was delivering pizzas and avoiding college. How well could he really be doing?

Still, Derrick decided to reach out.

When Sam picked up, he sounded genuinely happy to hear from him.

"Man, it's been a minute," Sam said. "How you been?"

"I've been alright," Derrick said. "I figured it's time we catch up. You down to meet up at the park? You know, our old spot?"

"Of course," Sam said. "Let's do it."

Reunited at the Park

The next afternoon, Derrick arrived at the park a little early, taking a seat on one of the swings like they used to as kids.

A few minutes later, he saw Sam pull up in a cab.

Derrick's first reaction was surprise. A cab?

Not just any cab, but a slightly beat-up, older model cab that looked like it had seen better days.

Derrick chuckled to himself. "Man, I guess things didn't work out too well for him after all."

When Sam walked over, Derrick greeted him with a smirk. "So, this is what you've been up to? I knew you were delivery pizza, but now you're driving cabs, I didn't know it was like that," he teased, motioning toward the cab.

Sam laughed and shook his head. "I see you're still the same, huh?"

Derrick chuckled. "Nah, I'm just messing with you. But for real, man, you sure you don't wish you went to college and got a degree?"

Sam grinned. "I'll answer that in a minute," he said. "But first, why don't you tell me what's been going on with you?"

Derrick's Reality Check

Derrick sighed. "Man, it hasn't been easy," he admitted. "I went to college, got my degree in business administration, and figured I'd land some great management job straight out of school. But you know what I've learned? A degree doesn't guarantee you anything."

Sam listened as Derrick vented about his struggles finding a job that paid well, about the reality of competing with thousands of other graduates, and about how he had bounced from one underwhelming job to the next.

"I started off managing a seafood chain," Derrick continued. "That paid me $40,000 a year. Not exactly what I expected after four years of college. Then I moved on to a communications company, managing a team for $55,000 a year. And even with that, after taxes, I barely see $1,000 a week."

Sam nodded. "So, are you happy?"

Derrick sighed. "Not really. I mean, I'm grateful to have a job, but man, it's hard. Long hours, limited freedom, and I still don't feel financially secure. I'm engaged now, and I want to buy a house, but I just don't see how I'll ever afford one on my salary."

Derrick shook his head. "But you know what? At least I have my degree. No one can take that from me."

Sam smiled. "And I'm proud of you, man. I'm really glad you went after what you wanted."

Derrick gave a small smile. "Enough about me, though. What about you? What have you been up to?"

Sam leaned back on the swing. "Derrick," he said, "I'm a millionaire now."

Derrick's Jaw Drops

Derrick burst out laughing.

"Man, if you're a millionaire, we're all millionaires!"

Sam just smiled. "I'm serious."

Derrick looked at him, suddenly realizing that Sam wasn't joking. "Wait... you're serious?"

"One hundred percent," Sam said.

Derrick's laughter faded into disbelief. "How? The last time I saw you, you were delivering pizzas. And now you're driving cabs? And you're telling me you're a millionaire?"

Sam laughed. "Yeah, it sounds crazy, right?"

Then, he broke it all down.

Sam told Derrick everything—his first real estate deal, the mentors who had guided him, the investments he made, how he had built a portfolio worth over million while leveraging other people's money and most importantly how he prayed to God to show him the way.

Derrick sat there, his mouth hanging open.

"Where did you get the money to do all this?" he finally asked.

Sam shook his head. "It wasn't about the money," he explained. "Yeah, I put some of my own money into things like appraisals and education, but really, it was about learning strategies and being creative with financing. It was about believing in myself and taking opportunities that most people ignored."

Derrick stared at him. "Man... I had no idea."

Sam nodded. "I know. And I'm not here to downplay your choices, but I will say this—you doubted me back then. You kind of laughed at me when I said I wasn't going to college, but all I really needed was some support."

Derrick looked down, feeling a little guilty.

"I found that support in Tony, the pizza shop owner, and Michael, the cab driver," Sam continued. "Those guys gave me insights that changed my life. I learned how to leverage the money I made, how to create passive income, and how to build real wealth. Now, even if I never drive another cab in my life, I'm set."

Derrick was silent for a moment, taking it all in.

"I've never heard this perspective before," he admitted. "I always thought college was the only way to success. But... you're living proof that there's another way."

Sam nodded. "Exactly. I don't trade my hours for money anymore—I let my investments do that for me. My real estate empire and my book, The Rich Cab Driver, generate money for me every day. I don't work for money anymore—money works for me."

Derrick's eyes widened. "Wait—you wrote a book?"

Sam grinned. "Yeah, almost a year ago. It's been selling like crazy."

"Can I get a copy?"

Sam chuckled. "Of course. Let me grab one from the cab."

He handed Derrick a copy, and Derrick took it with newfound respect for his old friend.

That night, Derrick started reading.

Three days later, his entire perspective on life had changed.

Biblical Perspective From the Author: True Prosperity Comes Through Wisdom and Faith

In this chapter, Derrick learns that his traditional mindset about success was limiting him, while Sam's willingness to seek knowledge outside of conventional paths led to financial independence. This contrast highlights a biblical truth—success comes not just from worldly education, but from applying wisdom and taking action in faith.

Ecclesiastes 7:12 (KJV): *"For wisdom is a defence, and money is a defence: but the excellency of knowledge is, that wisdom giveth life to them that have it."*

Derrick believed that a degree would automatically provide security, while Sam understood that financial success requires wisdom, strategy, and application. True financial freedom isn't just about what you know—it's about how you use that knowledge to create opportunities.

Additionally, **Psalm 37:23 (KJV)** reminds us: *"The steps of a good man are ordered by the Lord: and he delighteth in his way."*

Sam didn't follow the standard path, but he remained open to learning, seeking mentors, and trusting that God would guide his steps. Instead of limiting himself to the options society presented, he walked in faith and discovered a path that led to financial independence.

Finally, **Deuteronomy 8:18** (KJV) declares: *"But thou shalt remember the Lord thy God: for it is he that giveth thee power to get wealth, that he may establish his covenant which he sware unto thy fathers, as it is this day."*

Sam's story is a testimony to the fact that wealth and success come through God's wisdom and provision, not just human effort. When we trust in Him, seek wisdom, and take action on the opportunities He presents, we unlock financial freedom in ways beyond our expectations.

The lesson from this chapter is clear: True success is not just about education—it's about wisdom, faith, and obedience to God's direction.

Chapter 10 Notes

- What stood out to you in this chapter?
- How can you apply these principles to your own life?
- What action steps will you take moving forward?

Chapter 11

A New Path

Derrick couldn't wait to see Sam again.

After finishing the book Sam had given him, Derrick's entire perspective on money and success had shifted. He had spent the last three days devouring every page, realizing how much he never knew about wealth, leverage, and financial freedom.

So, as soon as he turned the last page, he picked up his phone and called Sam.

"Man, we have to meet up," Derrick said, excitement in his voice.

Sam chuckled. "I take it you finished the book?"

"Yeah, and my mind is blown. I have to hear more from you in person."

"Let's do it," Sam said. "Same place as last time?"

"Yeah," Derrick agreed.

Breaking It All Down

The next afternoon, they met up again at the park. Derrick barely let Sam sit down on the swing before he started talking.

"Man, that book was amazing. The details, the strategy—I had no idea this was even possible."

Sam nodded, a knowing smile on his face. "I get it, man. I understand. You were put in a position where you were taught that wealth and freedom could only be achieved one way—through college, a degree, and a corporate career. That's what the world tells everyone."

Derrick nodded. "Exactly. And here I was, thinking I was doing the right thing, but struggling to find financial security, while you—" He shook his head, still in disbelief. "Man, you figured out a way to beat the system."

Sam leaned forward. "To be honest, I resisted the normal path, but I didn't have all the answers at first. I just knew there had to be something else out there. And that's how I stumbled upon real estate, mentorship, and leverage."

Derrick listened closely, eager to soak up every bit of knowledge Sam was about to drop.

The Truth About Leverage

"One of my mentors once told me what leverage truly is, and that changed everything," Sam said.

"The reason why you're frustrated, Derrick, is because you have to make all of your money yourself. Think about it. You're calculating your salary, subtracting your expenses, and trying to figure out how to afford a house, a wedding, and a future—but you're thinking about it in terms of what you personally have to earn and save."

Derrick nodded. "Yeah… that's exactly how I think about it."

Sam smiled. "That's the problem."

Derrick frowned. "What do you mean?"

Sam leaned in. "The difference between me and you is that I don't have to work for my money anymore. I let my assets do the work for me. So instead of thinking, 'How much do I need to personally earn to afford something?' I think about what assets I need to acquire that will pay for what I want."

Derrick sat back, processing that thought.

"So," Sam continued, "you're looking at your salary and stressing over how you're going to afford a home and a wedding. I don't think like that at all. I just calculate how many more income-producing assets I need to cover the cost."

Derrick let that sink in. "Mannnn… so you don't even take on financial burdens—you just build income streams that handle them for you?"

"Exactly."

Derrick shook his head. "Man, I feel like I just got another degree—but this time, one that actually teaches me how to be free."

Sam chuckled. "You see, that's what they don't teach us. They tell us to work for money instead of learning how to make money work for us."

Derrick ran a hand down his face. "And now, I have to start from scratch."

"No, you don't," Sam said. "You're already ahead of the game. You just need the right strategy."

Derrick's Reality Check

For the first time, Derrick opened up about his real financial struggles.

"I have to be real with you," he said. "I'm drowning in student loan debt. I was so focused on getting my degrees, I didn't realize that I'd be in so much financial trouble when I graduated.

"Now, I'm stuck paying back all this money while trying to survive on a salary that barely allows me to build anything. My credit isn't great because there were times when I had to miss payments just to keep up with other bills.

"And to be honest, man, I don't even know if I can afford to get married at this rate."

Sam nodded. "I get it, bro. But here's the thing—you're not stuck. You just need a different approach."

The Mentorship Begins

Derrick looked at Sam, eyes full of hope.

"Man, I really need you to teach me what you know. I want to build what you built."

Sam smiled. "Of course, man. This is exactly what Tony the Pizza Guy and Michael the Cab Driver did for me. They helped me see the possibilities I never knew existed. And now, I'll do the same for you."

Derrick exhaled, feeling a sense of relief. "So where do I start?"

Sam leaned forward. "First, you need to set a goal to acquire your first asset. You need to get something working for you—something that generates income even when you're not working."

Derrick nodded. "That makes sense."

"Now, if you want to start with real estate, you need to understand something—most people think you need a lot of money to get started, but that's not true. What you really need is patience, strategy, and the right opportunity."

Derrick raised an eyebrow. "So, you're saying I can start without much money?"

"Absolutely," Sam said. "I didn't have hundreds of thousands of dollars when I started. I just found the right deal and structured it correctly. If you position yourself the right way, you won't need a lot of your own money at all."

"Okay, but how do I find these opportunities?"

"That's where networking comes in," Sam explained. "Letting people know what you're looking for, putting signals out into the world, and most importantly, believing that God will align you with the right deal at the right time."

Derrick smiled. "Man… this is wild. All my life, I thought working hard was the only way. But now, you're showing me how to work smart."

Sam nodded. "Exactly. You already know how to put in the work—you did it for your degree. Now, it's time to shift your focus to building wealth. And with leverage, the rewards are far greater."

A New Journey Begins

Derrick sat back, letting everything sink in.

"So, what's my next step?"

Sam grinned. "We start by fixing your credit and putting a real plan together. Once that's done, we find you your first deal."

Derrick felt a surge of excitement. For the first time, he wasn't just dreaming about a better future—he was taking action to build it.

And as they sat there, old friends reconnecting in a whole new way, Derrick knew one thing for sure—

His life was about to change forever.

Biblical Perspective From the Author: The Power of Transformation

In Chapter 11, Derrick begins to see the world differently after reading Sam's book. His perspective on wealth, financial freedom, and success shifts dramatically. This transformation aligns with a biblical truth: true change begins in the mind before it manifests in one's life.

Romans 12:2 (KJV): *"And be not conformed to this world: but be ye transformed by the renewing of your mind, that ye may prove what is that good, and acceptable, and perfect, will of God."*

Derrick had been conditioned to believe that success could only come from a college degree and a traditional job. However, Sam's journey showed him that financial freedom is possible through wisdom, strategy, and faith. Similarly, God calls us to renew our thinking, allowing His wisdom to guide our paths rather than simply following societal expectations.

This chapter encourages readers to seek God's wisdom in all areas of life and be open to the unconventional paths He may lead them on.

Chapter 11 Notes

- What stood out to you in this chapter?
- How can you apply these principles to your own life?
- What action steps will you take moving forward?

Chapter 12

The Idea That Could Change Everything

Sam and Derrick met up for lunch at one of their favorite spots. It had been a few weeks since they reconnected, and Derrick had been soaking up all the knowledge Sam had shared with him about real estate and financial independence. Today, however, the conversation took a different turn.

Sam leaned back in his chair, stirring his drink. "Derrick, I've been thinking a lot about something lately."

Derrick nodded, intrigued. "What's on your mind?"

Sam exhaled. "You know, I've been in this industry for years—between driving cabs, networking with independent drivers like Michael and the guys, and even riding with customers who share their experiences. I keep hearing the same complaints over and over."

Derrick raised an eyebrow. "About what?"

"About the big ride-share apps," Sam explained. "A lot of people don't like getting random drivers. They want consistency. They wish they could book the same driver they trust, instead of rolling the dice every time they need a ride. And the drivers? Most of them feel like they're being exploited, working long hours for little pay while the companies take massive commissions."

Derrick leaned in. "Yeah, I've heard similar things. But what are you thinking?"

Sam tapped the table. "What if I solved that problem? What if I created a service where passengers could choose their preferred drivers, schedule rides in advance, and keep their transportation more personal? And at the same time, we let drivers keep more of their money and use flashier cars?"

Derrick's eyes widened. "Man… that's actually a genius idea. You'd be fixing a real issue. But how would you even make that happen?"

Sam smirked. "That's what I was hoping you could help me with."

Derrick thought for a moment. "Well, I've met a couple of people who developed their own apps. Some of them got working prototypes made without breaking the bank. You might want to check out Fiverr. You can find freelance developers there who can create a working version of your idea."

Sam immediately pulled out his phone and made a note. "Alright. I'll check it out when I get home."

That night, Sam logged onto Fiverr and started searching for app developers. He found a handful of programmers who specialized in building mobile platforms. After reaching out and explaining his vision, he received several quotes—some as low as $5,000, others reaching as high as $40,000.

Sam had the money, but he wasn't about to throw $30,000 into something that might not work. Instead, he sent a proposal to a developer who quoted him $30,000.

He wrote:

"I'll give you $2,000 upfront, and instead of the full fee, I'd like to offer you a percentage of the subscription fees for three years—until we raise outside investment. This way, you're not just a hired developer; you're part of something bigger."

Three days later, the developer responded. "I'm in."

Sam was thrilled. This meant the project could move forward without him putting all his money on the line. He called Derrick the next day.

"Bro, we're in business," Sam said.

Derrick was just as excited. "Man, that's amazing! How can I help?"

Sam smiled. "You're already helping. Look, I know you were trained to work for big companies, but you have real skills. Skills that I need. This company is going to need structure, financial planning, and long-term strategy. That's where you come in. I want you as a partner."

Derrick blinked. "Wait, you're serious? It's your idea."

"I know," Sam said, "but business is about leverage. Your skills can help take this to another level. So, I want you to have 10% of the company. Besides, while we are waiting on the perfect real estate deal for you, we can focus on consistently building out this business for ourselves."

Derrick sat back, stunned. "Man, I don't know what to say."

"Say yes," Sam said with a grin.

Derrick chuckled. "Alright. Let's build this thing."

With that, their partnership was sealed. Sam was confident that they were about to create something massive—something that would not only change their lives but change the entire industry.

Biblical Perspective From the Author: The Power of Partnership and Problem-Solving

Sam's decision to partner with Derrick and pursue this business idea highlights a powerful biblical principle—God often provides opportunities for wealth through solving problems. When we stay attuned to the needs around us, we can create solutions that not only serve others but also bless us financially.

Proverbs 16:3 (KJV) states: "Commit thy works unto the Lord, and thy thoughts shall be established."

Sam didn't jump into this blindly. He carefully planned, strategized, and negotiated while trusting that his solution would meet a real need. His approach mirrors how faith and action work together—he took a leap of faith, but with wisdom and preparation.

Additionally, **Ecclesiastes 4:9-10 (KJV)** reminds us of the power of partnership: "Two are better than one; because they have a good reward for their labour. For if they fall, the one will lift up his fellow: but woe to him that is alone when he falleth; for he hath not another to help him up."

By bringing Derrick into this venture, Sam ensured that both of their strengths were being used to build something greater than what either could have done alone.

The takeaway here is clear: God often gives us ideas through the problems we notice—and when we act in faith, surround ourselves with the right people, and commit our work to Him, He establishes our plans.

Chapter 12 Notes

- What stood out to you in this chapter?
- How can you apply these principles to your own life?
- What action steps will you take moving forward?

Chapter 13

The Beta Test: Turning an Idea into Reality

The idea was taking shape, but Sam knew that having a great concept wasn't enough—it had to be executed properly. After all, businesses don't succeed because of ideas; they succeed because of action.

With the feedback gathered from drivers and passengers, it was time to move forward. The next step? Structuring the business properly.

Derrick took the lead on that. Sitting across from Sam in the small office space they had rented, he pulled out a stack of notes and placed them on the table.

"Alright," Derrick said, looking up. "We need to get everything lined up. A solid foundation. Branding. A revenue model. A plan for how this thing actually works. We can't afford to launch sloppy."

Sam nodded. "Agreed. We have one shot at a first impression. Let's get it right."

Derrick tapped his pen against the table. "So here's how I see it. The drivers? They need control over their income. No commissions taken from their fares, just a simple monthly fee to be part of the network. And passengers? They need certainty—they need to know who's driving them, when they'll be picked up, and what kind of experience they're getting. That's the whole appeal. That's what separates us from the big guys."

Sam leaned back in his chair, thinking it over. It was a clean, simple model. Instead of taking a percentage of every ride like the major ride-share companies, their platform would let drivers keep everything they made. The only thing they'd pay was a flat $29.95 per month to be listed on the app. Meanwhile, passengers would pay $9.99 per month for the ability to choose their own driver, schedule rides in advance, and ensure a consistent experience every time they used the service.

"You really put some thought into this," Sam said, shaking his head with a grin.

Derrick shrugged. "That's what I went to school for. Might as well put it to good use."

Sam chuckled. "And here you thought that degree was only good for working a nine-to-five."

Derrick laughed. "Hey, man, I'm just glad I can use it for something that actually benefits us both. Speaking of which—we need to test this thing before we go all in. I know you're confident in it, but we have to make sure the system works before we start charging people."

That made sense. If they were going to roll out the app nationwide, they needed proof of concept first. The best way to do that? A beta test.

The Beta Launch Strategy

Sam decided to start small—give people the chance to try it out with no commitment. He called it the 60-day beta test.

"We'll give the first fifty drivers free access," Sam explained. "No charge at all. Let them use the platform, build a customer base, and see how they like it."

Derrick nodded. "And what about passengers?"

Sam leaned forward. "First two hundred get free access for sixty days. No risk, no payment—just a chance to experience the convenience. If they like it, they stay. If they don't? No harm done."

Derrick scratched his chin, thinking. "That's smart. It removes any hesitation. Once people try it, they'll be hooked. And we can gather feedback along the way."

That was the key—feedback. Sam didn't just want users; he wanted insights. What worked? What needed improvement? What unexpected problems might arise?

By offering the beta for free, they could fine-tune the app based on real-world experiences, not just theory.

The First Sign-Ups

With the plan in place, Sam and Derrick got to work recruiting their first users.

The first step was going directly to the drivers Sam already knew—the guys who met every Saturday.

Michael was the first to sign up. He had been one of Sam's biggest supporters, and he knew the value of building a customer base rather than relying on random fares.

"I've been in this game for years," Michael said, tapping the screen of the phone as he signed up. "Having regulars changes everything. If this app can give me a steady group of riders, I'm all in."

By the end of the first week, twenty drivers had already joined the beta test. Most of them were experienced cab drivers who had long-time passengers but had never had a system that allowed them to lock in their regulars and schedule rides easily.

The next step was getting passengers onboard.

Sam started with his own customers—the people who called him directly for rides. Every time someone booked a ride with him, he brought up the app.

"I'm starting something new," he'd tell them. "A service where you don't have to worry about random drivers—you get to pick who you ride with, every time."

People were instantly interested.

"Wait, so I could just schedule all my rides with you and never have to deal with anyone else?"

"Exactly," Sam said. "And for the first two months, it's free."

One by one, riders signed up. Within three weeks, they had reached two hundred passenger sign-ups.

The First Hurdles

Of course, no business launch is ever smooth.

Just as things were picking up, technical problems started surfacing.

Some users struggled with the booking system—ride confirmations weren't always coming through properly.

A handful of drivers had trouble syncing their calendars, leading to missed reservations.

And some passengers weren't sure how payments would work once the beta period ended.

But Sam didn't panic.

"This is exactly why we're doing the beta," he told Derrick. "We're catching the problems now, before we go live."

They took detailed notes, made adjustments, and worked with the developers to fix every issue.

Over time, the system improved, and by the end of the 60-day period, the response was overwhelmingly positive.

The Turning Point

By the end of the beta test, 70% of the initial users wanted to continue—even if they had to start paying.

The demand was there. The app worked.

And now, it was time for the next step: the official launch.

Biblical Perspective From the Author: Planning and Preparation

Before fully committing to his rideshare platform, Sam took the time to test, refine, and adjust his vision. He gathered feedback, launched a beta test, and ensured the business model was sound before investing heavily. This mirrors a powerful biblical principle—taking wise counsel and making plans with foresight.

Proverbs 15:22 (KJV) states: *"Without counsel purposes are disappointed: but in the multitude of counsellors they are established."*

This verse emphasizes the importance of seeking advice, testing ideas, and refining a vision before launching something new. Sam didn't act alone—he sought insights from drivers, passengers, and business-minded people like Derrick. This process of wise planning ensured his success rather than failure.

Success isn't about rushing in—it's about aligning strategy, wisdom, and action with sound counsel.

Chapter 13 Notes

- What stood out to you in this chapter?
- How can you apply these principles to your own life?
- What action steps will you take moving forward?

Chapter 14

Finding the Perfect Name

After months of testing, tweaking, and refining the app, Sam knew that the final step before launch was branding. The beta testing phase had proven that both customers and drivers loved the idea, and now it was time to make it official.

But before he could take the business to the next level, he needed the perfect name.

Sitting across from Derrick at their usual lunch spot, Sam opened his laptop and pulled up a domain registration site.

"Alright," Sam said, rubbing his hands together. "Time to find a name."

Derrick leaned in. "So what are we going for? What do we want this name to say?"

Sam thought for a moment. "It has to be simple, easy to remember, and instantly tell people what we do."

The biggest rideshare companies in the world had one-word names—short, catchy, and powerful. But getting a single-word brand name would be nearly impossible.

"Two words max," Sam said, typing into the search bar. "Something clear, easy to say, and recognizable."

Derrick nodded. "And something drivers will be proud to work under."

Brainstorming the Names

For the next two hours, they brainstormed 25 potential names, checking domain availability as they went.

Here's what they came up with:

1. **RideSelect.com**
2. **DriveRight.com**
3. **MyDriver.com**
4. **CabChoice.com**
5. **DriverLink.com**
6. **RideSmart.com**
7. **TrustRide.com**
8. **GoDriver.com**
9. **CabSync.com**
10. **DirectCab.com**
11. **MyCabChoice.com**
12. **RideSync.com**
13. **PersonalCab.com**
14. **RideElite.com**
15. **SelectCab.com**
16. **GoCab.com**
17. **RideEase.com**
18. **DriveSync.com**
19. **PersonalDriver.com**
20. **TrustCab.com**
21. **PreferredRide.com**
22. **ReliableDriver.com**
23. **CabPro.com**
24. **CabSelect.com**
25. **PersonalRide.com**

As expected, most of the domains were already taken.

Sam sighed. “Man, finding the perfect name is harder than I thought.”

Derrick smirked. “Welcome to branding. It’s like real estate—good properties get scooped up quick.”

After narrowing it down, they found two strong names still available:

- PersonalCab.com
- CabSelect.com

Sam liked both names, but he wasn’t about to make the decision alone.

Surveying the Customers

“Let’s ask the people who will actually use it,” Sam said.

For the next two days, he surveyed 40 of his regular passengers—the people who had helped him grow his business.

The question was simple:

“Which name do you like better: PersonalCab or CabSelect?”

The results were clear—80% of customers preferred PersonalCab over CabSelect.

One passenger summed it up perfectly:

“PersonalCab just sounds like exactly what I want. A personal, reliable driver. It feels different from Uber and Lyft.”

Sam smiled. That was all he needed to hear.

Locking in the Name

Sam immediately went back to GoDaddy and registered PersonalCab.com.

"It's official," Derrick said as Sam completed the purchase.

Sam leaned back and smiled. "Now, let's turn this name into a movement."

With the name finalized, they were one step closer to launching the company.

Biblical Perspective From the Author: The Power of Planning and Seeking Input

Sam's decision to survey his customers before finalizing the company name reflects an important biblical principle: Wise leaders seek counsel before making major decisions.

Proverbs 11:14 (KJV) *"Where no counsel is, the people fall: but in the multitude of counsellors there is safety."*

Instead of making a rash decision, Sam took the time to gather insight from the people who would actually use the service. This ensured that the brand name would resonate with his audience and make a strong first impression in the marketplace.

Another powerful lesson comes from:

Ecclesiastes 7:8 (KJV) "Better is the end of a thing than the beginning thereof: and the patient in spirit is better than the proud in spirit."

This verse reminds us that success comes through patience, careful planning, and wisdom. Sam could have rushed into picking a name, but instead, he took the extra step to ensure the best possible decision.

The takeaway? Success isn't just about having a great idea—it's about taking the time to execute it properly and seeking wise counsel before making major moves.

Chapter 14 Notes

- What stood out to you in this chapter?
- How can you apply these principles to your own life?
- What action steps will you take moving forward?

Chapter 15

Scaling PersonalCab to a Multi-Million Dollar Business

Sam sat in his office, staring at the screen. After weeks of testing, countless conversations with passengers and drivers, and a deep analysis of user feedback, *PersonalCab* was no longer just an idea—it was a fully functional service with a solid foundation. The beta phase had gone better than expected, and with the confirmation that people loved the concept, it was time to take the next big step: branding and full-scale launch.

Creating the PersonalCab Identity

Before moving forward, Sam knew that PersonalCab needed a strong brand identity. A name alone wouldn't be enough—it needed a logo, a recognizable visual that would stick in people's minds.

He logged onto Fiverr again, just like he did when he first hired a developer. This time, he searched for logo designers. After browsing through dozens of portfolios, he found a designer whose work stood out. The designs were clean, professional, and modern—exactly the look Sam wanted for PersonalCab.

He reached out to the designer and explained the concept. Within 24 hours, the designer responded with a proposal:

- $250 for a simple logo with three different mockups to choose from.
- $500 for a premium package with unlimited revisions and branding elements.

Sam didn't hesitate—he went with the premium package. He wanted something perfect.

Within five days, the designer sent over the first mockups. Sam and Derrick reviewed them carefully, considering every detail. They wanted a logo that captured the essence of personalized, preferred, and professional rides.

After a few revisions, they landed on a sleek, modern design—a stylized P and C intertwined in a way that subtly resembled a steering wheel. It was simple yet striking. They loved it.

Now, it was time to move forward. Sam sent the finalized logo to his developer, giving him the green light to integrate it into the app. The branding was now complete, and PersonalCab had a polished, professional image.

The Strategy for Expansion

With the branding in place, Sam and Derrick moved on to expanding PersonalCab into the market. Their first focus was to onboard as many drivers as possible before opening the service to passengers on a larger scale.

They agreed on a two-step marketing approach:

1. **Recruiting Drivers**: The best way to grow was by targeting independent drivers—those who already had a customer base but wanted more control over their income.
2. **Onboarding Passengers**: Instead of targeting random passengers, they would allow drivers to bring their own customers into the system, making the service more personalized.

Driver Recruitment: The First Milestone

Sam and Derrick printed 5,000 marketing flyers, investing $150 into high-quality 4x6 cards that explained the benefits of joining PersonalCab. They hit the streets, handing them out to cab drivers outside airports, hotels, train stations, and private car services.

The results were instant. Within the first week, 1,500 drivers signed up.

By the second week, another 1,000 drivers joined.

By the end of the first month, over 5,000 drivers had joined the platform.

By Month 3, PersonalCab had 20,000 drivers signed up and fully using the app.

With drivers in place, it was time to scale the passenger side.

Passenger Growth & VIP Subscription Model

PersonalCab had already facilitated over 150,000 total rides within nine months. While some passengers used the free service to book rides, 25% of them upgraded to a VIP membership for additional perks.

The **VIP membership cost $9.99 per month** and gave passengers:

- Access to **exclusive drivers** with high ratings.
- The ability to **schedule last-minute bookings** without extra fees.
- Priority matching for peak hours.
- Special **luxury ride options**, such as **high-end black car services** and SUVs.

At 25% conversion, **37,500 passengers** upgraded to VIP.

Calculating PersonalCab's Revenue

With **20,000 drivers** onboarded and a **95% retention rate**, this meant:

- **95% of 20,000 drivers = 19,000 drivers** stayed after the free trial.
- **Each driver pays $29.99 per month.**
- **Total Monthly Revenue from Drivers:** **19,000 × $29.99 = $569,810 per month.**

From the **VIP membership** side:

- **37,500 passengers paying $9.99 per month**
- **Total Monthly Revenue from VIP members:** **37,500 × $9.99 = $374,625 per month.**

Total Monthly Revenue:

- **Driver Subscriptions: $569,810**
- **VIP Passenger Subscriptions: $374,625**
- **Total: $944,435 per month**

PersonalCab was officially a multi-million-dollar business.

Derrick's Gratitude & Sam's Vision for the Future

Sitting in the office one evening, Derrick looked over the numbers in disbelief. "Man… we're about to cross a million dollars a month," he said, shaking his head. "I never thought I'd be part of something like this."

Sam grinned. "That's what happens when you solve problems. We saw the gap in the market, and we filled it."

Derrick nodded. "And to think, I almost overlooked this opportunity. I was so focused on finding a corporate job, I never realized I could actually be an entrepreneur."

Sam laughed. "You don't need a suit and tie to build wealth. You just need the right strategy."

The two of them sat in silence for a moment, taking in everything they had built. The journey had been long, but this was only the beginning.

Biblical Perspective From the Author: A God-Given Blueprint for Success

Sam's story is a powerful reflection of how God gives people the ability to create wealth through wisdom and problem-solving.

In **2 Kings 4**, we see the story of a widow who had nothing left but a small jar of oil. The prophet Elisha told her to borrow jars from her neighbors and begin pouring oil into them.

Miraculously, the oil kept flowing until every jar was filled, providing her with a way to pay off her debts and live off the rest.

The lesson? God gives us opportunities to create wealth using what's already in our hands.

Sam started as a cab driver—an ordinary job. But through wisdom, innovation, and problem-solving, he turned that experience into a business that changed his life.

This chapter reminds us that God often places solutions to problems within our reach—but we must be willing to see it, act on it, and trust that He will bless the work of our hands.

Sam didn't wait for an opportunity—he created one. And because of that, his business grew beyond anything he ever imagined.

Chapter 15 Notes

- What stood out to you in this chapter?
- How can you apply these principles to your own life?
- What action steps will you take moving forward?

Chapter 16
The Big Exit

Sam had built something that was bigger than he ever imagined. What started as an idea discussed over lunch had turned into a multi-million-dollar business that disrupted the ride-share industry. PersonalCab had not only changed Sam's life but also the lives of thousands of drivers who now had full control over their earnings, and millions of users who enjoyed a more personal and predictable ride experience.

For the first year and a half, Sam and Derrick scaled PersonalCab organically, focusing on driver recruitment, marketing, and refining the user experience. They stayed independent and avoided outside investors, allowing the business to grow at a steady pace.

The Pre-Investment Success

Before institutional investors came in, **PersonalCab** had:

- **100,000 drivers**, each paying **$29.99/month** = **$2,999,000/month**
- **1.2 million users** on the platform, with **20% (240,000 users) upgrading to VIP** at **$9.99/month** = **$2,397,600/month**
- **Total revenue before institutional investment: $5,396,600/month**

Derrick was thrilled with their progress. "Why do we even need institutional money when we're already making over $5 million a month? We can stay private and keep growing," he argued.

Sam thought long and hard about it. "We could, but if we want to scale beyond New York, Chicago, and L.A., we need major funding to expand globally. Plus, institutional investors bring in more than just money—they bring influence, connections, and infrastructure. The faster we scale, the harder we'll be to compete with."

Derrick hesitated, but he knew Sam was right. They needed to take PersonalCab to the next level.

The Institutional Investment and Rapid Growth

After months of negotiations, a group of institutional investors offered $50 million for a 33% stake in the company, valuing PersonalCab at $150 million. The funding allowed them to:

- Expand into **25+ new cities** across the U.S.
- Improve their app's technology and **enhance driver support systems**
- Launch a **high-end VIP service** for luxury riders
- Increase their marketing efforts and **onboard 500,000+ new users per month**

Within three years of institutional investment, the company exploded in growth:

- **600,000 drivers**, now paying **$39.99/month** = **$23,994,000/month**
- **7.5 million users**, with **25% (1.875 million users) upgrading to VIP** at **$14.99/month** = **$28,106,250/month**
- **Total revenue after scaling: $52,100,250/month**

PersonalCab had become a dominant force in the industry.

The Buyout Offer

With the company now generating over $52 million per month, major competitors in the ride-share industry took notice. One of the largest ride-share corporations offered to acquire PersonalCab for $1.2 billion.

Sam and Derrick sat across from each other in their office, looking at the official offer.

"We really built a billion-dollar company," Derrick said, shaking his head in disbelief.

Sam nodded. "And now, we have a decision to make."

After careful discussions, Sam decided to sell his remaining stake in the company. By this point, he owned 62% of PersonalCab, while Derrick held 10%. After investors and early team members were paid, Sam walked away with $744 million, and Derrick cashed out with $120 million.

A Life Forever Changed

The sale was one of the largest exits in ride-share history.

Derrick, who once struggled in corporate America, now had generational wealth. Sam, who started as a struggling pizza delivery guy, was now a self-made billionaire.

As they stood in their office for the last time, Derrick turned to Sam. "So what now?"

Sam smiled. "Now, we build something else. But first, we enjoy what we've built."

Derrick chuckled. "You know… I never thought I'd say this, but I'm glad I left corporate America."

Sam laughed. "I told you, man. You don't work for money—money works for you."

They shook hands, knowing this was only the beginning of their next chapter.

Biblical Perspective: The Power of Vision and Obedience

Sam's journey mirrors the parable of the talents found in Matthew 25:14-30 (KJV). In this passage, a master entrusts his servants with talents (money), expecting them to multiply what they have been given.

- One servant **invests and doubles his talents**, receiving great rewards.
- Another servant **hides his talent out of fear**, and it is taken from him.

Sam had every reason to doubt himself. He had no college degree, no major connections, and no guarantee that PersonalCab would succeed. But he took the talent and opportunity given to him and multiplied it into something life-changing.

This is a powerful lesson:

God gives each of us gifts, ideas, and opportunities. It is up to us to use them wisely, take action, and trust that He will multiply our efforts.

Just like Sam, when we act in faith, apply wisdom, and take strategic risks, we open the door for unimaginable blessings.

The Legacy of The Rich Cab Driver

Sam's story is more than just a business success—it's a blueprint for financial freedom.

- He **invested in real estate** and built long-term wealth.
- He **wrote a book** that inspired thousands.
- He **built a billion-dollar company** that changed an industry.

Sam didn't follow society's definition of success—he created his own.

And that is the true power of vision, faith, and action.

The End

Chapter 16 Notes

- What stood out to you in this chapter?
- How can you apply these principles to your own life?
- What action steps will you take moving forward?.

Epilogue:

The Truth Behind *The Rich Cab Driver*

Most people assume that success follows a straight path—graduate high school, go to college, get a degree, land a high-paying job, and live happily ever after. But real life doesn't work that way.

The truth is, there are many roads to financial freedom, and the path that worked for me isn't the one society told me to take. That's why I wrote *The Rich Cab Driver*—to share an alternative reality that so many people overlook.

Between 2003 and 2005, I drove a cab, and during that time, I had some of the most life-changing encounters of my life. It was a season of transition, where I was figuring out my purpose and meeting people who unknowingly shaped my future. That's where this story comes from.

Although Sam and Derrick are fictional characters, their journey represents the real choices, struggles, and breakthroughs that shaped my own path.

My Story: Why I Chose a Different Route

When I graduated high school, I opted out of college.

At the time, it felt like I was doing something wrong because everyone around me kept saying college was the only way to succeed.

- **"What are you going to do with your life if you don't go to college?"**
- **"You're going to regret it if you don't get a degree."**
- **"You'll never make good money without higher education."**

I heard these statements constantly. The pressure was real.

But here's the thing—I already had an entrepreneurial mindset, even before I knew what that meant. The problem? I didn't have the right people around me to encourage me or to show me what was possible.

Why College Isn't the Only Way

Let me be clear: I'm not against college.

If you want to be a doctor, lawyer, or engineer, college is necessary.

But for many people, it's not the only way to success.

And the idea that you can't be successful without a degree is a lie.

There are other ways to build wealth, and in many cases, those ways are better suited for people who aren't meant to sit in a classroom for four years, accumulating debt.

For me, the key to financial freedom wasn't a degree—it was knowledge, strategy, and mentorship.

My First Mentors Changed Everything

One of the biggest turning points in my life was meeting my first real mentors.

Until then, I had no guidance, no clear vision, and no understanding of what it took to become wealthy without working a traditional job.

My mentor introduced me to a concept that changed my life:

Leverage.

Before that moment, I had never heard that word in a financial sense. I didn't know that wealth isn't about how much money you personally make—it's about what you do with it, how you multiply it, and how you position yourself for long-term success.

That's why I made sure to weave that lesson into this book.

- **Leverage in real estate.** Learning how to buy **assets** without needing a fortune upfront.
- **Leverage in knowledge.** Turning what you **know** into income, whether through **books, courses, or mentorship.**
- **Leverage in relationships.** Building a **network of successful people** who can open doors and help you grow faster than you ever could alone.

These lessons didn't come from a classroom. They came from real-world experience, trial and error, and learning directly from those who had already made it.

How This Book Mirrors My Life

This book isn't just a motivational story—it's a reflection of my real experiences.

Like Sam, I spent time driving a cab.

Like Sam, I made millions with my own Internet domains

Like Sam, I eventually built a real estate portfolio.

And like Sam, I made my biggest leap forward when I purchased a commercial building—a property I acquired for just under $1 million, which is now one of my greatest financial assets.

That investment, along with other properties and income streams, is what makes me a millionaire today.

The Growth of PersonalCab: A Real Business Model

In *The Rich Cab Driver*, Sam took an industry problem—the lack of stability and control for independent drivers—and built a billion-dollar company that gave drivers more power over their own income.

The PersonalCab concept isn't just fiction—it's a real opportunity.

In fact, I registered PersonalCab.com while writing this book because I believe this idea can become reality.

This isn't just about storytelling.

It's about showing people how to spot a problem, create a solution, and turn it into generational wealth.

Wealth Isn't Built Overnight

There's something people need to understand:

Wealth takes time.

It doesn't happen overnight. It doesn't happen by accident.

Even the Bible tells us:

"The plans of the diligent lead surely to abundance, but everyone who is hasty comes only to poverty." – Proverbs 21:5

That's why patience is key.

You have to set your goals, chip away at them, and be consistent.

And most importantly, you have to renew your mind.

"Do not conform to the pattern of this world, but be transformed by the renewing of your mind." – **Romans 12:2**

If you want different results, you have to think differently.

Final Words of Advice

If you take one thing away from this book, let it be this:

You don't have to work for everything you get. You can build assets that work for you.

The sooner you start thinking this way, the sooner you can create the life you truly want.

- Find **mentors** who have already done what you want to do.
- Take **small but intentional** steps toward financial freedom.

- Stop thinking you have to do **everything on your own—leverage is the key.**

I hope Sam's journey inspires you to look at your own life, your own ideas, and your own potential differently.

Because the truth is, *The Rich Cab Driver* is not just Sam's story.

It could be yours.

Other Books by Allen Brown

Become a Millionaire Before 50

Discover the Five-Fold Disciplines That Can Make You a Millionaire Before 50

What does it take to reach millionaire status before the age of 50? This book lays out the blueprint, showing you step-by-step how to build wealth, create passive income, and secure financial freedom—no matter where you're starting from.

At the heart of this guide is the Five-Fold Disciplines, a powerful framework designed to accelerate your path to wealth:

- **Mindset** – Transform the way you think about money, shifting from scarcity to abundance.

- **Principles** – Master the financial habits that create lasting wealth, including consistency, planning, and reinvestment.
- **Leverage** – Learn how to multiply your income through scalable systems and passive revenue streams.
- **Mentorship** – Unlock shortcuts to success by learning from those who've already walked the path.
- **Faith** – Stay resilient and trust the process, even when obstacles arise.

Why This Book is a Game Changer:

Unlike traditional financial guides, *Become a Millionaire Before 50* doesn't just focus on making money—it teaches you how to **strategically position yourself for long-term wealth, financial independence, and a legacy beyond your lifetime.**

Through **personal experiences, proven strategies, and real-world examples**, Allen Brown reveals how he built multiple businesses, leveraged real estate, and overcame obstacles to achieve financial success.

Start your millionaire journey today. Your financial freedom begins with the right disciplines!

Million Dollar Seed: How My Last $17,600 Grew to Millions God's Way

What happens when you take your **last $17,600** and entrust it fully to God? *Million Dollar Seed* is a **powerful story of faith, obedience, and divine provision**, revealing how one man's financial struggles transformed into a testimony of **God's supernatural blessings**.

This book isn't about **get-rich-quick schemes** or financial shortcuts—it's about **spiritual alignment, patience, and trusting God's timing.** Allen Brown shares his personal journey through **three pivotal phases** of spiritual growth:

- **Life before Christ** – Navigating struggles, financial uncertainty, and self-reliance.
- **Faith Awakening** – Learning to trust in **God's provision and promises** despite doubts.

- **Walking in Divine Favor** – Seeing faith in action and experiencing **financial breakthroughs** led by **God's guidance.**

Rooted in **biblical wisdom** and **real-life application**, this book draws lessons from Abraham and other faith leaders who trusted God against all odds.

This isn't just a financial success story—it's a **faith-building guide** that will inspire you to:

- **Surrender your fears and finances to God.**
- **Discover how faith can lead to true prosperity.**
- **Learn how obedience unlocks divine blessings.**
- **Experience peace, joy, and fulfillment beyond money.**

If you've ever faced financial setbacks, uncertainty, or doubt, *Million Dollar Seed* will strengthen your faith and show you how to plant seeds for a future of abundance—God's way.

Escape The Rat Race God's Way

Discover Biblical Secrets That Can Unlock Your Path to Financial Freedom

Are you tired of the daily grind, living paycheck to paycheck, and feeling like financial freedom is just out of reach? *Escape the Rat Race: God's Way* is not just another financial book—it's a spiritual roadmap that reveals how biblical wisdom leads to lasting wealth and fulfillment.

Inside, Allen Brown breaks down seven key biblical principles that serve as the foundation for true prosperity:

- **Faith** – Trusting God as the ultimate provider.
- **Obedience** – Aligning your actions with biblical financial wisdom.
- **Sacrifice** – Understanding delayed gratification to build wealth.
- **Wisdom** – Making smart financial decisions based on **timeless biblical truths**.
- **Resourcefulness** – Maximizing what you have and creating multiple streams of income.
- **Gratitude** – Shifting your mindset from scarcity to abundance.

- **Generosity** – Unlocking **God's blessings** through giving.

This book challenges society's definition of success, showing you that true wealth is more than just a number in your bank account—it's about financial stability, spiritual growth, and living a life of impact.

Whether you're feeling trapped in a **9-to-5 routine**, struggling to get ahead financially, or searching for **God's plan for your financial future**, this book will give you a **fresh perspective on money, work, and success**.

Inside, you'll learn:

✓ How to break free from the **cycle of financial stress** and live with **abundance.**
✓ Why applying **God's financial principles** leads to **supernatural increase.**
✓ How to shift from **working for money** to **making money work for you.**
✓ Practical steps to **escape the rat race** and step into **financial independence—God's way.**

This is more than just financial advice—**it's a life-changing experience.** If you're ready to embrace **God's plan for financial freedom**, *Escape the Rat Race: God's Way* will show you the **path to abundance, joy, and peace.**

Your journey to financial freedom—God's way—starts now!

Your Life Is Not A Coincidence

Your Life Is Not a Coincidence reveals a powerful truth: the events in your life are not random—they are part of a greater design. This transformative book introduces the **3 Pillar Perspective**, a framework that uncovers the hidden forces shaping your reality: **God's Hand**, **Conscious Decisions**, and **Subconscious Influence**.

Through personal stories, timeless wisdom, and practical insights, you'll discover how divine guidance, intentional choices, and unseen beliefs work together to create the outcomes you experience. You'll learn to recognize when God is moving in your life, make decisions that align with your purpose, and overcome subconscious patterns holding you back.

This book is your guide to understanding life's deeper meaning and taking control of your future. Nothing is by chance. When you embrace the 3 Pillar Perspective, you'll see that your life is divinely connected, purposeful, and filled with potential.

About the Author

Allen Brown is a relationship coach, author, and speaker with over 20 years of experience helping individuals and couples navigate the complexities of love, trust, and communication. Drawing from his personal journey of a 27-year marriage, Allen brings wisdom, empathy, and actionable insights to his writing, offering practical tools for building stronger connections and understanding the deeper issues that impact relationships.

As the founder of **Allen Brown Ministries** and **Build Our Kingdom Publishing**, Allen is dedicated to ministry outreach and publishing transformative spiritual and relationship-focused books. His journey with Christ began in 1998 during a life-changing Easter morning service, shaping his mission to help others apply godly principles in relationships and personal growth.

Through his books, workshops, and counseling, Allen empowers women to recognize unhealthy patterns, strengthen their relationships, and walk in faith-based wisdom to create a fulfilling love life.